NEEDLE

TO THE NORTH

Edited by William C. James

ARTHUR C. TWOMEY

ISBN 0 88750 457 4 (hardcover)
ISBN 0 88750 458 2 (softcover)

Cover illustration from a photograph by A. A. Chesterfield, taken about 1902 at Great Whale River, courtesy of Queen's University Archives. Book design by Michael Macklem.

Printed in Canada

PUBLISHED IN CANADA BY OBERON PRESS

INTRODUCTION

In *Needle to the North* Arthur C. Twomey's story of an expedition to subarctic Quebec in 1938 becomes, almost inadvertently, a classic narration of the journey-quest. What might have been merely a straightforward account of a scientific expedition takes on mythological overtones. The "precious object" to be found and brought back is a specimen of a fresh-water seal, known by the Inuit of Hudson Bay as *kasagea,* and distinguished from its salt-water counterpart, *netchek,* the common ringed seal. *Kasagea,* if not quite the white stag or unicorn of ancient legendary quests, approaches that kind of mythical status in Twomey's story. In 1935 J. Kenneth Doutt, Curator of Mammalogy at the Carnegie Museum of Pittsburgh, had noticed at Great Whale River a sealskin bag hanging from an Indian's shoulder. The bag appeared to be made from the skin of a hair seal, though not that of *netchek* nor, indeed, of any hair seal known to science. "Does the layman understand what the sight of a piece of strange sealskin means?" asks Dr. Twomey. "It means the clue to possible discovery of a new large mammal, and the discovery of any new large mammal is now so rare that even the possibility gives a scientist the jitters."

According to the Indian the strange skin had come from the Seal Lakes region of the Ungava interior, more than 100 miles inland from Hudson Bay's Richmond Gulf, and about 800 feet above sea level. For years these lakes had been thought to contain seals, a possibility intriguing to biologists. And, during the preceding 30 years, the Carnegie Museum had sent numerous expeditions to the Hudson Bay region in its attempt to chart the complete natural history of the Labrador Peninsula. But Doutt's encounter with the Indian and his strange sealskin bag led directly to the launching of an expedition in 1938 to search for the mysterious *kasagea* of Seal Lakes.

Arthur C. Twomey, who had just completed his Ph.D. in biology at the University of Illinois, was Doutt's companion on the expedition. As Assistant Curator of Ornithology at the Carnegie Museum Dr. Twomey had his own scientific interests, separate from those of Doutt, and was assigned by the Museum the project of going to the Belcher Islands for the spring bird migrations. Anyone acquainted with the life and work of the film-maker, Robert Flaherty, will know about his "discovery" of the Belcher Islands. Though only about 60 miles from Hudson Bay's east coast, these barren, rocky and wind-swept islands had almost no contact with civilization until well into this century. They remained unexplored, their size and extent officially unimagined on the govern-ment maps and charts that acknowledged this chain of islands, hundreds of square miles in area, as but a mere pinpoint until Flaherty's visit there in 1914. In the same year Claus J. Murie, a Carnegie Museum biologist, had spent ten days on the Belchers. His reports persuaded others that a full scientific investigation of the place needed to be conducted.

The fulfilment of this hope was delayed many years until the plan was made to combine in a single expedition the winter journey to the Ungava interior for the strange seal and the scientific investigation of the Belcher Islands in the spring. The search for the seal, *kasagea*, was to be finished in time for the party to cross the unreliable ice-bridge from the mainland at Great Whale River to the island of Tukarak among the Belchers. As Twomey put it:

> Our alliance was one of expediency; we would accomplish in eight months — not in the two years necessary were each treated as a single expedition — both our separate, yet interrelated projects. To James Bay by train. To Moose Factory, Rupert House, Fort George, Great Whale River Post, by dog sled. Then inland by dog sled to the Seal Lakes region of Ungava, to secure a specimen of the strange fresh-water seal. Then out again (of course with our specimens), and across the ice jam to the Belcher Islands, just in time

6

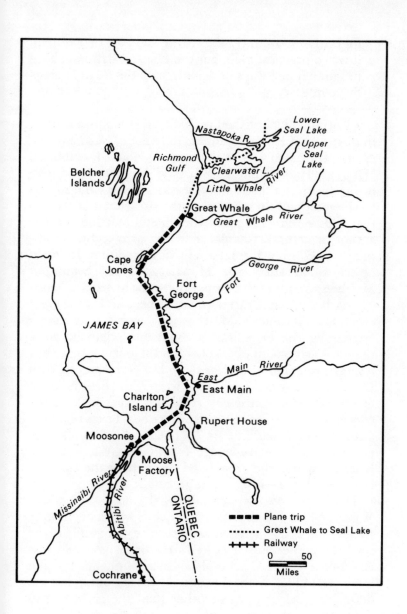

for bird migrations in the spring. Laid out on the map, it was a practical plan, but the Hudson Bay east shore has unmapped ways of dealing with the feasible plans of people.

As originally published in 1942, by Houghton Mifflin in Boston and Herbert Jenkins in London, *Needle to the North* consisted of two parts. In Part 1, subtitled "Ungava (Hudson Bay, East Coast)," Twomey recounted, in the form of a quest story, the search for *kasagea,* the fresh-water seal. In many ways the situation is similar to that in *The Snow Leopard,* where Peter Matthiessen, the author, a naturalist-explorer in his own right, accompanies "GS" on a formal scientific expedition. Its main object is to study the Himalayan blue sheep, but Matthiessen hopes to glimpse the snow leopard, a "near-mythic beast," and "rarest and most beautiful of the great cats." Like Twomey's, Matthiessen's narrative is less an account of the expedition's ostensible scientific goals than it is an account of another kind of journey, more like a pilgrimage. Part 1 of *Needle to the North* began with Doutt the mammalogist and Twomey the ornithologist leaving Pittsburgh the day after New Year's, 1938, and concluded with their return from the Seal Lakes region to Great Whale River. In Part 2, "The Belcher Islands," the party crossed the ice-bridge from Great Whale to the Belchers where they remained throughout the summer until the ship *Dorothy* came to collect them.

The difference between Parts 1 and 2 is marked. Whereas Part 1 is the story of a quest, with a beginning, middle and end — a narrative structure — to unify it and hold it together, Part 2 lacks a structuring device such as the journey. The Belcher Islands account, quieter and more reflective than the search for *kasagea,* has no definable goal or purpose other than the gathering of data and the observation of birds on the Belcher Islands. The result is that it is less a *story* and more a series of meditative or anecdotal observations of nature (includ-

8

ing, as in Part 1, *human* nature) in all its aspects on these remarkable islands. The impression is of timelessness, with only the changing of the seasons and of the weather as a reminder of temporality, until the arrival of the ship and the end of summer bring the account to a close. Twomey says, thinking of the Belchers ("probably the last stronghold of the ancient Eskimo world") and of the lone white man there: ". . . I want to go on writing only of Tukarak, of the dogs, the pipits, Markisee and summer, and the big canoe; to live in my mind only for *oblu,* which is one day, or at most for *oblu macook,* which is two, and to forget that other days are coming for the people of the Belchers — bitter days, the days of *mana,* the many tomorrows."

No doubt this poetic, almost mystical, lament is in part Twomey's expression of sorrow over what took place on those islands between the time he left and the time of writing — the massacre of nine Inuit in 1941, the result of religious hysteria and messianic claims. Perhaps because Twomey came along chiefly for the Belchers part of the expedition, he is there free to observe and to record without needing to find a narrative form by means of which to shape his writing. Though Part 2 is to be commended for its own particular qualities, and not least for its anecdotes of people, there is difficulty in seeing how Parts 1 and 2 of *Needle to the North* as originally published belong together. Especially if Part 1 is considered as a literary structure, Part 2 does not seem to provide a necessary and effective conclusion. For these and other reasons, but principally because Part 1 is an integral unit, the decision has been made to reprint only Part 1 of *Needle to the North.* The account of the journey-quest, the search for *kasagea,* stands on its own.

A mythic beast requires a mythic country to inhabit, and Twomey almost creates such a place in the region he typically calls "Ungava." Now known as Nouveau-Québec, Ungava stretches east from Hudson Bay to the Labrador boundary, and north from the Eastmain and

Hamilton Rivers to Hudson Strait. Twomey described it as "bigger than Texas and as stormy as Cape Horn" and "guarded by wind, snow and natural violence of every sort." Acquired by Canada as part of the Hudson's Bay Company Territories, Ungava was for a time after 1870 incorporated into the Northwest Territories, and then administered separately until in 1912 it was granted to the province of Quebec. For almost a century travellers along the East Main (that is, the east coasts of Hudson and James Bays) have left accounts of their journeys. The result is continuous and extensive documentation of various travels along the East Main coast and to the Ungava interior.

Until the turn of the century almost the only whites living there were Hudson's Bay Company traders and Anglican missionaries. Then, gradually, geologists, government parties, surveyors, rival traders and scientists began to venture up the coast. In most instances the usual method of access to the east shore of Hudson Bay, and thence to the Ungava interior, was to travel from the railway by canoe down the Misssinaibi or Abitibi Rivers to Moose Factory, and then to make one's way by canoe, York boat, small coastal ship or dogsled around the foot of James Bay and north up the East Main coast. Except for the fact that they were able to travel by rail to Moosonee, Twomey and Doutt expected to make their journey by similar means. Though most of their food and equipment had been transported to Great Whale River the previous summer on the annual supply ship, a month-long journey by loaded *komatik* from Moose to Great Whale was still (so they anticipated) required before the expedition could really begin.

Seen as the record of a journey of exploration or as the account of a scientific expedition, *Needle to the North* has its literary predecessors in such books as *A Summer and Winter on Hudson Bay* (1912) by the Leith brothers; *In Canada's Wonderful Northland* (1917) by William T. Curran and H. A. Calkins; and *My Eskimo Friends* (1924)

10

by Robert Flaherty. If *Needle to the North* is known and cited at all, it is usually by anthropologists or by historians of the Ungava region who have turned to Twomey's account for details of native life and of travel, for a description of the natural history of the area or for information about the Hudson's Bay Company's posts and personnel at Moose Factory or Great Whale River. Approached in this way, the account of the Carnegie Museum expedition of 1938 is similar in many respects to the description and narratives of earlier journeys. In fact, this winter journey to the Seal Lakes had never been done before by white men. In 1884 A. P. Low, the geologist and explorer, had been driven back after penetrating the interior only 45 miles. While Flaherty had crossed the Labrador Peninsula by dogsled 25 years before Twomey and Doutt, he had travelled across the open tundra, not at or below the tree-line. But except among those readers who already had reason to be interested in the Ungava region, *Needle to the North* has never received the attention it deserves.

In 1942, when it was first published, the minds of many Canadians were of course occupied with great events on the other side of the ocean. And, as Dr. Twomey himself has suggested, the appearance in the previous year of an account of life in the Arctic by Gontran de Poncins, *Kabloona,* overshadowed the publication of *Needle to the North.* Still, *Needle to the North* is a remarkable omission in the otherwise exhaustive summary of the previous year's publications in the April 1943 number of the *University of Toronto Quarterly* (see "Letters in Canada: 1942," ed. Philip Child, pp. 305-88). In a category devoted to "Narrative and Descriptive Writing about the Canadian Scene" not only were such books as *Canada Moves North* by Richard Finnie reviewed, but also Vilhjalmur Stefansson's *Greenland.* Meanwhile, in the section on "Fiction," it was lamented that there was a "common lack of interest in the Canadian scene and contemporary life as imaginative material." In

11

fact, with the single exception of the Hudson's Bay Company's quarterly publication, *The Beaver,* which had in 1939 published two articles by Twomey on the expedition, no Canadian magazine or periodical seems to have given *Needle to the North* any notice or review at all. But while the *Queen's Quarterly, Maclean's, Saturday Night, Canadian Forum* and the *Canadian Geographical Journal* ignored *Needle to the North,* the *New York Times Book Review* praised it in a 400-word review (3 May, 1942). There the reviewer seemed especially taken by this account of a journey to "virtually unheard-of places," speaking of the search in "that strange wilderness" and of its "human drama." The neglect within Canada is puzzling considering the reports that had come out of the Belcher Islands in 1941 of the religious massacre there, resulting in the deaths of nine Inuit people, a tragic event that led to articles in the *Queen's Quarterly, Maclean's* and even *Life* magazine. Part 2 of *Needle to the North* was of course not only concerned solely with the Belchers, but also contained a full portrayal of one of the perpetrators of the killings, Peter Sala, as Twomey had known him in the days before those terrible events of 1941.

For whatever reasons — a preoccupation with the war, the vagaries of book distribution in Canada, the fact that the Americans and the British a generation ago seem to have found the Canadian north more exotic and fascinating than Canadians did themselves — *Needle to the North* has never been known in this country as it deserves to be. Yet there are other reasons for bringing out a new edition at this time. On occasion it happens that a book appears before there is a suitable reading audience ready for it, or else it is presented to a public other than the one to whom it ought to be addressed. What was originally an account of a scientific expedition consisting of two related projects and intended for a mass audience in the United States and Great Britain can, with only the slightest adjustment, be seen today from a different perspective as the story of a quest, set within Canada, and having mythological overtones.

"The Quest is one of the oldest, hardiest and most popular of all literary genres," according to W. H. Auden. Others, such as Northrop Frye and Joseph Campbell, claim the quest story is central to all literature and mythology, and perhaps to human experience too. In its familiar form the quest tells of a hero's journey from a known world into the unknown, there to find a precious object — perhaps the Waters of Life or a beautiful princess or the Holy Grail. Along the way the hero encounters obstacles, undergoes tests and (if all goes well) succeeds, thanks to the assistance of certain helpers with their special knowledge and magical powers. If the "precious object," the mythic beast *kasagea,* is the goal of the quest, and if there is the painstakingly primitive journey by dogsled, toboggan and snowshoe to find it, how does "that strange wilderness" become a suitable locale, an unknown region, for these adventures?

The quest is supposed to involve a journey from the familiar world into an unknown realm. Homer's Odysseus did not have to leave the Mediterranean to have strange adventures. But as the boundaries of what is known have been pushed back, authors have had to take their questing heroes to increasingly remote places. In the early eighteenth century Jonathan Swift could simply send Gulliver to the other side of the globe. By the nineteenth, Jules Verne was sending men to the bottom of the sea or the middle of the earth or the moon. In the early part of this century other planets were the settings for the unfamiliar and the exotic. But it is doubtful, with the kind of knowledge we now have about the solar system, that the planet Venus, for instance, could serve as the location for fantastic adventures. Authors have therefore resorted to an imagined "other world," sometimes with links to this world (as in Narnia), at other times existing completely on its own (as with Tolkien's Middle-earth).

13

With increased exploration and scientific knowledge, then, most settings for unusual adventures and heroic quests have been used up. Perhaps, with the loss of community and the emphasis upon the solitary individual in an age of psychoanalysis and narcissism, the real adventures now take place within, the descent into the self having become the true heroic quest of the twentieth century. In fact, one critic has claimed that the history of literature since the Renaissance could be entitled "The Discovery and Colonization of Inwardness." But *Needle to the North,* perhaps with an anticipation of the "post-modern," is a quest story with a terrestrial setting: there is no journey to another world, nor a descent into the depths of the self. Like some other recent versions of the quest narrative, *Needle to the North* finds the strange and exotic in what lies close to hand. (Not that Ungava was very accessible in 1938.) Perhaps Twomey — who was born in Midland, Ontario and grew up in Alberta — responded to Ungava somewhat as James Houston did on his first visit to the same region ten years later: " 'You've been looking for this place all your life,' he told himself. 'And — this is the crazy thing — you're just north of where you were born. It's not Tibet. This is Canada. *Your own country!* " (Charles Taylor, *Six Journeys: A Canadian Pattern* [Toronto: Anansi, 1977], p. 75). What might be termed the "domesticization of the quest" can be illustrated from a recent book, *The Starship and the Canoe,* which describes the separate quests of a father and son. The father, a physicist of international reputation, was preoccupied with schemes to colonize the planets with a gigantic starship; his son, meanwhile, with a kind of counter-cultural atavistic wisdom, built a modern-day version of an Aleutian ocean-going kayak to travel the British Columbia coast.

Other ingredients of the traditional journey-quest are present in *Needle to the North.* The goal must be accomplished within limits set by restricted resources of food, the uncertainties of the weather, dissension among the members of the party and (at times) the reluctance of the native guides and hunters. And, as in other stories of the type, early success leads to unfounded and premature optimism. Twomey describes the elation he felt after he gained a whole month's travelling time when he and Doutt and George Moore (their guide and interpreter) are offered a chance ride by plane from Moosonee to Great Whale River. Then, true to the formula, frustrations and delays set in. They lose the month gained by an enforced wait at Great Whale, as the storms rage outside and their earlier plan of travelling by dogsled to the Seal Lakes proves unfeasible. It becomes necessary to alter the plans made in the south, before they knew the country; chagrined and humbled, they adjust to these new conditions. Throughout these delays — and others to come — Twomey learns to accustom himself to Ungava, to a world, as he puts it, governed by the sun, not the wheel.

The outcome is doubtful almost to the end, and the reader is kept wondering if the quest for *kasagea* will be fulfilled or not — and even if *that* goal is achieved, whether the return to Great Whale River will occur too late to make the trip to the Belchers. The inexorable passing of time and their inability to make haste are at certain points almost intolerable to Dr. Twomey, especially since his principal concern is with the expedition's second project. What if they get back to Great Whale (empty-handed or not) only to find it is too late to make the crossing to the Belchers on the precarious ice-bridge? While the narrative never becomes deeply introspective, the outer journey is paralleled by various stages of inner growth and development, as in *The Snow Leopard* (though without the presence of a philosophic apparatus such as Zen Buddhism and, of course, set in northern Canada rather than Tibet). The story remains an account of an external quest, set in an actual place, and never becoming a metaphor for something else. Twomey seems always to be aware that he is telling a story. Never, as with Pirsig's sometimes interminable "Chautauquas" in *Zen and the Art of Motorcycle Maintenance* or Matthiessen's meditative musings in *The Snow Leopard,* does the inner journey take over and assume the centre of attention. While Dr. Twomey is self-conscious to the extent that he can relate what is transpiring within, his awareness of his own subjectivity never becomes self-absorption.

As a narrator who is both an involved participant and yet sufficiently detached as an observer, Twomey is the ideal guide to take the reader on this Ungava quest for *kasagea.* His healthy objectivity is evident in his capacity to render the concrete particulars of the richly figured pattern in this expedition. Memorable are the fascinating details of bird life in the north, the descriptions of *komatiks,* snowshoes and toboggans and their uses, the arrangements for the setting up of camps and for meals, and the differences between the posts at Moose Factory and Great Whale River — all these ingredients keep us firmly fixed in the outer world of the quest itself. And out of such careful observation, accurate rendering and factual detail the archetypal aspects of the mythic quest grow naturally and organically.

As Clifford Wilson, editor of *The Beaver,* astutely observed in his review, though Twomey is a biologist "it is with human beings — Eskimo, Indian and white — that the book is chiefly concerned" (Sept. 1941, p. 41). Clearly Dr. Twomey likes people, and likes observing people, their habits, their characteristic ways of being. *Needle to the North* is a treasure-house of such incidental and anecdotal relations as the story of the soda and the beans, or of the baking of the apple pie. Capable too of turning the joke upon himself, Twomey is aware of the comic in the midst of the often bleak native life in the north. Though he may at times betray impatience and frustration, Twomey reveals his admiration for the natives as readily as he does his exasperation. Though he may at times be critical, his overall attitude is one of acceptance, of understanding and of healthy good humour.

The dominant impressions the narrative conveys are of the land and, just as powerfully and memorably, of its people — of Norman Ross, of Daniel and Luc, of Boyshish and Jacob Rupert, and of course of Ekumiak, the coast Eskimo brought along for his expertise as a seal hunter. Like his dog, Ekumiak is apparently superfluous in the interior country of the Indians. Yet it is Ekumiak, more than any other individual, who summons his resources to bring about a crucial turn at the darkest hour. As the suspense builds toward the end, time is running out and spirits are at their lowest ebb. Then, Ekumiak, like so many of his predecessors in the quest story, proves to be valuable in an unexpected way, displaying abilities quite different from those for which he was chosen. His pantomime in the Indians' tent at Seal Lakes has a magically transforming effect, and is decisive in determining the outcome of the quest. As Twomey writes: "I went back to my tent and to sleep, somehow purged of those dreadful emotions that had beset all of us the last few days. The situation had not changed, but I had. And so apparently had the Indians."

Beyond that let it be left in doubt for the time being how it all comes out, for this is one of those stories to be read for the very good reason of finding out what happens next (and what happens last). Unless, of course, this is one of those quest stories (*The Snow Leopard* is an example) in which by the end an inner adjustment takes place to the extent that it finally ceases to matter whether or not the questing hero catches a glimpse of the mythic beast. For the seed of this doubt is planted in the reader's mind: will the quest be a "success" in the literal sense or not? But before we reach that outcome, let us remember that "much more demands a place in the story first," as Twomey wrote in the first chapter of the earlier edition. "If you follow this tale . . . you will only hunt and hunt through the white hills of Ungava for a mysterious

17

kasagea, as the Eskimos call it, a strange fresh-water seal."

Finally something should be said about the changes made here to the earlier edition published in the United States by the Houghton Mifflin Company of Boston. Chapters 2 through 17 (pages 9-164) of that edition have been reprinted with very few changes even of a minor kind. The original first chapter, which served to introduce both Parts 1 and 2 in the 1942 edition, has been omitted, though the essential background from it has been incorporated into this new Introduction. The spellings of place-names have been changed to their modern equivalents (the Wiashtewan River is now the Wiachuan River). Otherwise, the names themselves remain as Twomey knew them in 1938 (and as they had been known for decades before): therefore Great Whale River has *not* been changed to Poste-de-la-Baleine, nor Clearwater Lake to L'Eau Claire Lake, nor the Richmond Gulf to Lake Guillaume-Delisle. But, although English names have been corrected where the earlier edition was in error ("Mavor" should have been "Maver," for instance), the names of the native people have been left as Twomey had them.

Both Twomey and his companion, J. K. Doutt, spelled the names of the Inuit and Indians as they sounded to them, occasionally verifying the spelling with Norman Ross, the HBC post manager at Great Whale. Sometimes Doutt and Twomey do not agree: where Twomey has "Ekumiak," Doutt has "Egomea" with "Kumiak" in parentheses. While Twomey had "Petacumeshcum," Doutt wrote "Petacameshcum." An anthropologist who did fieldwork at Great Whale River in 1949-50 spelled Daniel's surname "Patakamiskan," while today the family name has been fixed as "Petagamskum." Similarly, "Luc Cache" would be "Luke Kash," and "Kooke," "Cookie." Because the spellings, then, of the names of native people, both Inuit and Indian, have been fluid and variable until quite recently, it has been thought best simply to leave them as recorded by the author.

Consistent with informal usage of a generation and more ago, Dr. Twomey was accustomed to referring to the Indians around Hudson and James Bays as Swampy Crees. Today that designation tends to be reserved for the Cree living in the lowlands to the west of James Bay and Hudson Bay from the Moose River north to the Churchill River. The Cree Indians living on the east coasts of Hudson and James Bays, from the Nottaway River to the Richmond Gulf, are now regularly referred to as Eastern Cree (or East Main Cree). Accordingly, "Swampy Cree" has been changed to "Eastern Cree" throughout. Twomey used both the term "Eskimo" as well as "Innuit" (the term preferred today, though now spelled "Inuit"). His usage has been left as he wrote it, except that "Inuk" (the singular form of "Inuit") has been substituted where clearly one individual is referred to.

On the title-page of the original edition the name of "Nigel Herrick" appears as a collaborator with the author. Perhaps a pseudonym ("Nigel" is usually a masculine given name), she was the wife of an English professor at the University of Illinois and helped Dr. Twomey prepare *Needle to the North* for publication. While undoubtedly she contributed something — how much is difficult to ascertain — to the literary quality of *Needle to the North,* still it is Twomey's response to the land and its people that the story records, and through his consciousness that it is mediated. The concluding paragraphs of the introductory chapter of the original edition are worth quoting in full, not only because the information contained there is vital to understanding the expedition and its locale, but just as much because they illustrate well Twomey's abilities of observation and description:

One question inevitably arises at any discussion of the Ungava expedition: Why didn't we seek for *kasagea* in the summertime? It would, of course, have been quite possible to go inland on a summer expedition, but far less easily, perhaps, than you imagine. Few people realize that sub-Arctic summer has hazards almost equal to those of winter. Potentially, the summer sub-Arctic is a slough of mud. Like a saturated sponge, the land yields water at a touch. There are lakes, swamps, rivers, in every summer valley. There are bare rocks, waterfalls and lichen on the hills. Between the hills, inescapable pools, bogs, muskegs and soggy-floored evergreen forests occupy the plains (and probably the hilltop plateaus). Like oozings from an overloaded mop, the melting snow runs out into countless ponds that never sink below the pitted surface. The summer sun returns Ungava briefly to insects, birds and animals. Even the Indians largely desert it. Canoes are the only boats capable of shooting the fierce Ungava rapids, and of accommodating the half-ton of food, clothing, work and camp equipment such as we should have been forced to transport even in summer. But on a waterways expedition all boats and loads must frequently be carried on men's shoulders across boggy portages and around torrential waterfalls. Ungava summer, moreover, like winter, is a very uncertain season. I have seen a severe snowstorm on Hudson Bay at the end of July. To have sought *kasagea* in summer would have left undone all the winter bird work which I, as an ornithologist, deemed so important a part of the Ungava expedition. Any scientific work in Ungava, except along the banks of streams, must be accomplished when the ground is frozen, for only then may one walk freely over the countryside. It was necessary, furthermore, to be in Ungava in winter if we were to combine the Ungava expedition (at a great saving of time and money) with our second expedition, the summer research on the Belchers.

The Seal Lakes of Ungava lie in transitional territory from trees to tundra (or "bush to barrens," as

Northerners say), where much is still to be learned. How could men live there — get wood, meat or shelter? What living things survived there the whole bitter year? They were vital questions. For me, Ungava was to add a new chapter to my endless study of man's dependence upon birds. When *noraluk* (meaning the-birds-that-flew-over) first cast shadow of wings upon Tukarak, I must of course be there; but in the meantime, I thought, while ranging the icy uplands of Ungava upon the mystery of the strange seal, further research, perhaps of great significance, might also be accomplished.

A fine example of the factual detail and descriptive power by which Twomey evokes the ambience of the quest, these lines introduce to us the characteristic voice (matter-of-fact, often lyrical, always reassuringly knowledgeable) of the man who will be our narrator and guide during this trek through the snowy Ungava fastnesses.

WILLIAM C. JAMES

"THE SPECIAL"

Beyond Cochrane, commercial city of lumbermen, there are no more villages, only green coniferous forests, mile-markers instead of stations, and whining saws—the lumberman's universe. The Special is a logger's freight, with one black rickety wooden coach for passengers. It runs twice a week from Cochrane to the James Bay settlement of Moosonee, a new village that came in with the railroad.[1] Just across the Moose River, and opposite Moosonee village, lies the ancient Moose Factory Fur Trading-Post belonging to the Hudson's Bay Company. Like many trading-posts, it lies, for shipping convenience, on an island. (Where there are no good islands, posts usually are located at the mouth of a river.) At the Moose Factory Post we would pick up our guide and would continue to Great Whale River Post by dog sled.

We boarded the Special in the razor cold of the January dawn, tumbling from our hotel beds just in time to make it. My breakfast had been one scorching gulp of coffee, taken on the run. The track was piled with snow that mounted into high white banks on either side of us, shouldered aside by the snowplough attached to our engine as we slowly chugged along. It promised us a painful advance.

Inside the coach we were transported at once into old frontier Canada, to red plush, polished mahogany, oil-burning glass lamps with fragile tall glass chimneys (the lamps set into metal brackets along each wall), wire package baskets high overhead and filled to overflowing with paper sacks and cardboard boxes. But the people themselves did not fit into the gilded age of plush and polish. They all wore the clothes typical of their kind — the men in mackinaws, knit toques, high boots and mittens; the women distinguished from the men by rough, serviceable been-to-Cochrane browns and blacks. And it was guttural Quebec French that we heard on every side. Talk, talk, talk incessantly!

To our surprise, the car was crowded. Children raced in the narrow aisle, and long before noon there was the unbearable rattle of lunch-boxes being opened, explored and tied up again. Too late we realized that we should have brought food with us, for even in the first hour it was obvious that the train was relatively getting nowhere. The Special does more than carry the passengers; rudely, and at once, it initiates impatient outsiders into a land attuned, not to the wheel, but to the sun.

Slowly, strugglingly, as the snows deepened, mile-markers crept across our vision. Fogging, grunting, clouded with steam, the little train parted the thick drifts in a weary routine—stop, back, clear, get a running-start, lunge, jerk, jolt, hiss—while billows of whiteness rolled across the dirty windows, blinding the eyes to whatever else might have been seen. From dawn to four o'clock in the afternoon (about ten hours of travel), we waited hopefully for Mile 52. Mile 52 had been described as "a waiting-station."[2]

When at last we reached it, gnawingly hungry, we bundled up and dismounted in great expectation, but we must have been slow. Not one of the passengers was visible. Nor was there any station. Scattered along the tracks were a dozen or so frame buildings, and our ears were pierced with the loud, plaintive shrilling of saws. Mile 52 was only a lumber mill.

The cookhouse and bunkhouse were so appallingly snowcovered that eaves and chimneys seemed only to be peeping at us. Thin blue smoke rose straight and slowly from the two big chimneys, to hang suspended in a spreading circle above each roof, and each chimney was encircled with a dingy patch of tar-paper (revealed where the snow always melts away first). Fresh yellow sawdust on a great white hill showed the many white mounds about the place to be dust piles. Idle machines stood here and there in white grotesqueness. And before one of the larger shacks, drifted house-high, with clearance but at

23

the path and the windows, there suddenly stood a man, beckoning to us.

"Come into the cookhouse, fellows," he called out genially, "for coffee and cakes!" His name was Weeks. He was the owner of the mill.

The cookhouse, perhaps 30 by 70 feet, was full of crude long tables and benches, beyond which stood a chest-high partition. Behind the partition was the kitchen range and the cook in all his glory. Steams rose about him, but Cook wore the heavy grey flannel shirt of a lumberman. Our stomachs were devastated by the odour of baking sugar and the aroma of long-boiled coffee. Over Cook's head were hung the heavy kettles; piles of bread loaves, plates of cake and tins of pie were stored on the higher shelves. Something bubbled on the stove and was stirred at intervals. It was wonderful. In loggers' land, they tell me, a cook has got to be good, and especially with pastry, or the loggers will not stay! A good cook is always respected.

Mr. Weeks had a polite tone when he asked, "What ja got for these men?" and Cook, without acknowledgement, began at once to take down plates. Padding the handle of his fat old coffee-pot, he filled our cups to the brim, and then took time to look at us with a cheerful middle-aged grin. The pie was raisin! He slammed it onto the table, already cut, uttering his first and only words: "Jump to it!"

We jumped. We stood beside the hot, round-bellied, black iron stove and lived again. We didn't quite eat the whole pie; it was heady stuff, and we were no longer a part of *the land of the doctors.*

Lumber was not Mr. Weeks' only enterprise. He had a thriving second business operating chartered planes. I was astonished. Bush-pilots now make light of flying from Edmonton up to the Arctic Yukon, but wind-ridden Ungava is supposed to be a more hazardous matter. Weeks' offer to us was breathtaking. From the mill at once, straight up to Great Whale River Post, for $350! We could scarcely believe it. We had allowed a month's

24

time to get us from Moose Factory Post up to Great Whale River, and expected to spend $400, and to suffer all the risk and exertions of a long hard journey. But what was the use of excited talk and fast-beating pulses? Weeks' light plane could have taken us, but our load was much too heavy. That was all there was to it! Bitterly disappointed, we tried to return to our first enthusiasm for dogs and sled. "Good old dogs! They're safer, anyhow!"

It was almost suppertime, and workmen began to tramp singly, silently, past the window, with bright red socks turned down over the tops of their shoes and brilliant wide wool sashes, with lurid stripes in red, blue, green and yellow, wound dramatically around their waists.

Only Weeks and the mill manager and the cook seemed not to be French. Transition country, full of transition people! The lumberjacks, bold-eyed, black-eyed, silent and frankly curious, outstared us as we watched them. We were moving north.

One hundred and twelve miles of the train trip remained after Mile 52. But beyond the mill, Weeks told us, the track was clear. We would make it now, he said, speaking lightly, "at breakneck speed!"—meaning in about five hours.

We made it in eight, a wonderful eight, passing through mile after mile of spruce forests with blue-green branches theatrically draped in snow. What few passengers there were now grew quiet. Riding through such scenes, anyone would be quiet. The woods were utterly still. In open stretches the snow swept outward in immaculate prairies, and in the small groves that began to take the place of continuous forest land the whiteness lay unbroken, as fluid as shadows, under the trees. Only once in a great while the footprint of a rabbit or weasel showed where life had lately been.

In a torpor of pie, I let my mind relax and float where it would, sitting with closed eyes, after dark came, trying

25

to get a little rest; but for me it was a kind of secret home-coming to the sort of country I had known so long, and once so well. Half-dozing, I returned to my boyhood among the lakes and rivers and forests of central Alberta, where I had wandered with Big Frank Farley, my teacher in the ways of the wild things of Nature. Often in the dead of winter, we two—a small boy and a man—had walked ten miles through frozen forests to watch the swift dash of a goshawk as he pursued a ruffed grouse, or to hear the loud clear hammer of a big pileated wood-pecker as he drove his heavy chisel-like bill into a frozen stump. Then, as spring broke the chill of winter and the first returning mountain bluebird hunted for insects along the warm southern exposure of the hillsides, now bare of snow, we used to dream of more distant fields.

Even in the busy years at the university, with the first rush of spring and examinations over, Frank and I were off to the muskegs of the Athabasca country—hunting for the little-known nesting grounds of the greater yellow-legs. In rapid succession our hunting grounds widened, until one blustery evening just before sunset, Frank, my father and I stepped from the platform of a mixed freight as it came to a wheezing halt. The men on the platform were big, bronzed, red-checked fellows dressed in parkas and heavy winter clothes. They eyed us with interest, but kept their distance. Beyond the station the land was devoid of trees, a barren plain cut by dark, age-worn, rock ridges. Toward the east the muddy glow of a vast expanse of water reddened with the sun's last rays. It was my first glimpse of Hudson Bay! Fort Churchill! The barrens gounds — the summer home of hordes of migrating sandpipers, plovers, curlews, ducks, geese—a land to stir the soul of any ornithologist! We were there at last.

Men of science, already familiar with the port of Churchill, may be surprised to learn how much difference there is between the west and east coasts of Hudson Bay, but I had heard tales of east-coast desolation all my life.

To be sure, the west coast of Hudson Bay is lonely and primitive, despite the Government grain elevator and the single track of railroad (laid on top of quaking brush piles) and the boarding-house of Mildred from the Klondike, but compared with the east coast—the coast of Ungava—Churchill is a veritable Monte Carlo.

On the east coast there are no boarding-houses. On all the thousand-mile length of the east coast there is not a single white man's village. The Hudson's Bay Company and a few free traders provide the only "civilized" people to be seen there—and they are few indeed; beyond Fort George, even the missions have only native "ministers." A traveller in Ungava must carry everything in with him, and he almost forgets what he is travelling after because he must be so much concerned about his food.

Even the Indians and Eskimos to be found on the east and the west coasts of Hudson Bay are unlike. West-coast *coppers,* the caribou Eskimos of central Canada, with girlish hair-bobs and dickey-flaps on their parkas, resemble the Eskimos of Greenland, but they are not much like the Ungava cake-eaters—as most post-protected Eskimos everywhere are called. There is no such thing in the world as just an Indian, or just an Eskimo. The Hudson Bay shores are highly unsociable, and so extensive that a great variety of living conditions and even of climate have preserved there a great variety of native people.

What a Hudson Bay native is depends entirely upon his specific locality, a fact seldom realized about the east coast until one has been there. Does he have wood from trees, or only the vine-like sticks of the tundra, or nothing at all except rocks, water, snow and the mechanical aids provided by the Hudson's Bay Company? What food must he eat, what winds must he meet and what white men, if any, does he know socially? These are always the controlling factors in native life, and many tribes of differing habits and dialects belong to Hudson Bay East, the coast of Ungava.

There is a natural reason for east-coast separateness. The east-Bay coast has always been isolated behind masses of reefs and reefy islands, and it is probable that on the east coast the reign of that pitiless Ungava triumvirate, Scarcity, Hazard and Solitude, never can be bought to an end. Lying in long knife-blade formations, roughly ten to 60 miles offshore, these gigantic outcroppings of rock and iron, and Heaven only knows what other minerals, gloomily guard the Ungava mainland, stretching in an awesome procession 500 or more miles long. The Belcher Islands form a part of this dangerous and imprisoning wall.

The ocean current, which brings a sea-life to the west coast, is of no help to the coast of Ungava. The current enters the Bay along the western shore, touching at Churchill, but it does not return to the sea along the eastern coast as would be expected. Deflected by the line of reefs and islands, it returns to the sea outside them, leaving the east coast to contend with a backwash of treacherous minor currents, resigning it to submerged rocks, jutting reefs, late-floating ice fields, hanging fogs, sudden squalls, rimy autumn sleet and the blasting winds from the berg-laden Davis Strait. These winds sweep southward and westward across the whole of Ungava, with no predictability whatever, summer and winter. The east coast meets that wind squarely, and suffers tremendously from it.

There is nothing to do when it comes but seek cover, if it be nothing better than a snow cave or a boulder, for the dry grit of the surface snow is driven at hurricane speed and cuts the face like sand. Slopes of rocks stand black and polished afterward, cleared of every trace of snow. Frozen rivers are new-brushed, and the birdless, creatureless land awakes after the wind passes, as from a long sleep, voraciously hungry. Men reckon time in Ungava on the Hudson Bay coast as "after the last ground-drifter." Ungava exists by rule of winds.

The moisture from Davis Strait, with which the north-east wind is always laden, means that the temperature rises as the wind does, but men in the Ungava wind will always prefer the still, dry comfort of 50 below. The airplane may someday destroy the present east-coast walled isolation, but the Ungava of bad winds will never go.

The sea has had but little influence on the east coast of Hudson Bay. No boats at all, except the annual Hudson's Bay Company supply boat (bringing another year's store of food and trade goods to the post and carrying off the accumulated furs) and the Government doctor's boat in its annual survey of the ills of the natives, are expected on the Ungava east-Bay coast from one year to another. Out of the mysterious fastness of the interior, the Ungava Indians always emerge in summer and congregate on the coast for the short open-water season. Elated with the sun, the sight of the sea and each other, they perch on the sandy flats built up by tide action at the mouth of the Great Whale River, and, like rustling birds that mean to stay but a moment, they cluster in peaceful droves along the Hudson Bay shore.

They have come in their canoes soon after break-up, portaging from lakes to rivers, riding swift currents that swirl the inland waters downward with falls and rapids from the Ungava hills. Near the Great Whale River Post, the inlanders for generations have set up their summer teepees. Cooking-fires smoke before each tent. Without noise or commotion, with ready smiles and eyes full of expectation, they wait—hunting and fishing in the deep waters of the Bay, foraging in the rocky coastal hills for blueberries.

They wait for the doctor's boat with its Red Cross flag flying. They crowd to the wharf to welcome the *Fort Churchill,* the boat that brings visitors and Company supplies, silently shaking hands with the bishop or missionary, listening to preaching in "boss language" (interpreted by Old Harold, the interpreter, who rumbles out an inflectionless thunder of words from the Eastern

Cree dialect), learning hymns to sing together—"Jesus, Lover of My Soul." Waiting to be made much of! Confirmed, perhaps, with a laying-on of hands, or married even! (Perhaps to the same woman as last year.) Waiting for the sun to grow coppery, with sand-coloured clouds in flecks on the horizon, like dead leaves on a tent in autumn. Waiting until summer is over. . . .

When nights chill and the ground hardens, the teepees one by one disappear. The inlanders are returning to the mystery from which they came. Before October, the sand-plain lies smokeless, bleakly swept by a sleety rain. A running edge of ice outlines the shore each morning, freezing every night, breaking up every day with splinter and tinkle and a heavy slosh of waves, until presently there is a hard white edge that is no longer breaking. Floating blocks of ice strike the frozen edge and are sometimes held fast, great rough chunks frozen into the ice field that is ever widening and thickening.

Ice forms early within all land angles, for wherever a tongue of rock juts sharply out from shore, the extended point catches up quantities of floating blocks which, driven landward by wind and currents, tumble and pile upon each other in huge high walls. All day in late autumn, the ice blocks are crashing and breaking with indescribable sounds. Every hour the tumbled wall is being washed with spray that nightly freezes and welds the broken pieces into one. I have seen these ranges of ice standing, by midwinter, as much as 50 feet high. They rise up not only at the land angles on the shore, but also in many places out on the open surface of the Bay, for tumbles of blocks are sometimes deposited upon the smooth edge of the ice field while it is still forming, and there they become incorporated into the frozen plain and rise up from the surrounding whiteness like miniature mountains. Thus are formed the great "pressure ridges" so typical of the Hudson Bay scene in winter, whose peaks, casting long pointed shadows, make the Bay such

an eerie place to travel on, so awesome a place, so picturesque and so difficult to ride a sled over.

Our train reached Moosonee at midnight and ground to a
screeching stop that roused us from our fitful sleep. Dim
lights from a trainman's lantern showed us little more
than another mile-marker and a frame shed for the
housing of checked luggage. It was 25 degrees below zero.
Our guide was at the train steps—George Moore by
name, a white man. I liked him instantly.
　George Moore was important. His voice would be
heard through all the days of crises that were bound to
rise. Through his eyes, almost literally, we should be
seeing Ungava. He was young, strong and quiet-
mannered, neither fawning nor officious. He had been
recommended as a notable cook. He spoke the Swampy
Cree Indian tongue (the dialect used around Moose
Factory), also a "good" English, and knew a little, as we
later learned, about the east-coast vocabulary of Eskimos.
His wife was a full-blood Cree Indian, and although only
28, George already had four children.
　We stood talking, Doutt and I cut with the cold.
Opening our dufflebags on the spot, we got out our store-
bought parkas and our heaviest mitts, put them on
hurriedly and then walked off with George into starry
heavens—for between earth and sky there seemed little
distinction. We were sharply aware of the cold in our
faces, and of the sounds of crunching ice underfoot. It was
the end of all rails. They did not end in any blaze of glory.
Civilization had just dwindled away.
　We walked the quarter of a mile to the heart of the
little settlement, meaning the Moosonee hotel. We had
been prepared for life in the wilderness, but the handsome rustic room that we entered had chintz curtains,
slip-covered upholstery and a bright fire leaping in a
great stone fireplace. After mile-markers, forests and
wastelands, the Moosonee hotel was nothing short of a

31

miracle. It might be the banquet before the hanging, I thought, but certainly it *was* a glory at the end of the rails.

MOOSE FACTORY POST

"Why, that's no sled!" we said, looking from our dining-room window the next morning just after breakfast. "That's nothing but a *mikiapi!*"* It was only about five feet long, and harnessed to it were three little mild-mannered dogs, now resting before the overturned *komatik.*** It was overturned to keep the dogs from running away with it. George had been talking wind gauges with our hotel proprietor (the only man in the hotel in winter), who also operated the weather station. The sled proved to be not for us, but for luggage, and the animals were a source of shame to our guide.

"Got the makin's of a good team here," he said ruefully, "if I had another set of ten dogs!"

George knelt on the sled himself, ludicrously, but in apparent comfort, grasping the sides to keep from falling off. East-coast sleds are simply rough platforms, without handles, back-rests or any fancy Alaskan devices. The dogs were hitched in fan formation, the only one possible in the rough Hudson Bay country. The lead dog pulls on the longest line, far in front of the others; the boss dog pulls nearest the sled and in the midst of the rest. Each dog is on a separate leash, free to find his own level, and the lines are of varying lengths. On Hudson Bay east coast the general rule for a full-sized pack is 66 feet for the line of the lead dog and six feet less for every dog that comes after.

With George kneeling on the sled and Doutt and myself walking, our little procession cut through the settlement, past the Company store (supplementary to

*Eskimo word for model, or miniature, toy (East coast and the Belchers).
**Eskimo word for sled.

32

the store on the island), past the store of the one free-trader, and past four or five drift-banked white frame houses, standing bleakly in pious separateness. We followed two wide rutty treads of a caterpillar tractor, which had brought supplies from the island to the settlement, meeting no-one, seeing no movement except the few swirls of snow that rose and settled at our feet. The sky was clear, the air knife-like; my skin already felt lightly starched. It was exactly 30 below zero.

"Indians," murmured George helpfully, when we passed low wooden shacks with slow-smoking rusty stovepipes for chimneys.

As prearranged by George, an agile, gay young fellow opened up the depot for us, reminding me of the talkative passengers on the Cochrane Special, for he jabbered like a magpie. Where were we going; what were we North for; was it a *real* expedition; what were our real nationalities (for I am dark, strongly resembling my French mother, and Doutt with a little blond goatee has a Scandinavian look to him). Especially, wouldn't we call on him socially later, for talk, for tea, for anything so long as we would give him a little company! But our guide was cold to all proposals, I noticed.

"A bachelor," George commented distrustfully, when we had loaded our sled with essential luggage and moved on and away.

Had we stepped out of our trail anywhere, we should have floundered in deep soft snow. A tarpaulin covered our cases and with the load lashed evenly George could still ride, but he dismounted where the trail pitched down the river bank. The dogs, fleeing from the fast sled following, twisted their way among humps of rocks and willows while all of us ran too.

Trails criss-crossed the river everywhere. We chose the widest. Once a black-shawled Indian woman plodded distantly past us and an Indian man passed later. While we were walking, the slight wind stung our faces, but we were otherwise comfortable.

33

"Why don't you freeze to death?" we once asked George, who laughed without answering. We each wore two pairs of wool socks (one light and one heavy), two suits of wool underwear, flannel shirt, canvas parka and very thick wool trousers; but George wore only a light pair of wool pants, with overall pants over them, a dark blue post-store sweater (with a wide red stripe running around its middle), mitts, like ours, and only a round toque on his head. We wore caps that we had brought with us, and after a little while pulled up the full-circled hoods of our parkas and felt like a couple of drab-coloured Saint Nicks. Perhaps George's wife had had a hand in his costume, for Indians, in sharp contrast with Eskimos, are notoriously underdressed.

It was three miles from Moosonee to the Moose Factory island, a calm, crisp, monotonous little walk over the frozen Moose River. We talked little, for under the double covering of cap and parka hood it was hard to hear. Before us spread the fan-stretch of leashes, each with a jiggling black dog at its end, and beyond the dogs lay the darkly forested shore of the river, marked vaguely by the line of a great spruce tree that had fallen athwart the bank and halfway into the stream.

I realized gratefully that a bright sun would have turned the snow, now only crystalled, into a blinding vastness of glitters. Even as it was, when I occasionally took a turn kneeling on the sled, I rested my eyes by gazing into the dark folds of the tarpaulin.

Within half an hour we had gained the edge of Moose Factory island, confronted by a steep climb among clumps of spruce and willows, while the little dogs barked and the one larger dog whined nervously. With a sharp word, George started them upward. We followed cautiously, keeping well in the track.

"Drifts are bad here," warned George, calling back to us. "Over your head probably."

At the island edge we took breath and our bearings. We were still a mile from the Moose Factory trading-post (on the opposite side of the island), and we must cross through the fine island forests to come to it.

"Indians!" said George again, pointing to the many footpaths trampled out by snowshoes. "Hauling wood for Company fires!"

We came up to the Moose Factory settlement from the rear, the size and age of the store revealing the ancient importance of the place. Moose Factory, a noble relic, was once chief factory for the whole east coast of Hudson Bay. Higher than the roof of the store flew the Hudson's Bay Company's historic bright flag (mounted, I surmised, between the two cannons so often seen in pictures). The soundless trail that skirted the store brought us eventually around to the front of it. The clearing was immense. Surrounding the white frame buildings of the post proper was a brown freckling of raw wood shacks belonging to Indians, and adjoining the post clearing was a white-steepled Anglican mission church surmounted by a cross. All was lonely and imposing and lifeless, and absolutely silent. Not until we had actually entered the store did we see anything of the manager, the Scotsman named Cargill.

Busy, cheerful, middle-aged and disinterested, Cargill shook hands with us, his pencil tapping the counter and his mind plainly on something else. Did we sleep well? Was the hotel comfortable? Wouldn't we be better off to move at once to the post-house? Mrs. Cargill had a room ready for us. Wouldn't we like to prepare for cold weather? He was looking doubtfully at our shoed feet.

Our clothes, ordered last summer from Winnipeg, waited for us in his attic, and we all went there at once, where I selected heavy wool shirts, heavy wool underwear, wool pants, duffle-socks and Indian moccasins— the Indian *winter* moccasin with high canvas tops to keep snow out. Next, Cargill took us to see our room in his dwelling and to present us to Mrs. Cargill.

She too was from Scotland, pretty, cultured and with many talents. For her, isolation seemed a pity. The

Cargill house was the typical dwelling of the Hudson's Bay Company, white frame with red trimming, and with a veranda to protect the front door. Inside there was almost nothing to distinguish it as frontier household, except that in the central hall (from which the living-room led off on one side and the dining-room on the other) hung a beautiful all-white parka of thin silk-like balloon cloth, the hood made heavy with a great circle of spotless white fox fur.

I don't remember when I first saw Mrs. Cargill wear this typical Northern woman's dress, but I shall never forget the sight of her in white parka, long blue pants and gaily decorated boots and mittens. Not only was she a white woman in the land of Indians, but she wore superbly well the strikingly beautiful costume, duplicated a thousand times the North Country over, having as its origin utility and utility only, treating a woman more as man than woman, yet extremely feminine in its effect. The white fox fur encircled her face. Red roses were embroidered around the bottom of the parka, and bright bits of embroidery in red, blue, purple and yellow richly splashed the boots and mittens. I remember her as she so often stood against the outer wall of the post-house, an amazing warmth in that frozen waste.

The first day grew steadily colder. The temperature dropped from 30 below in the morning to 35 below in the afternoon. At four o'clock, Cargill brought us a rumour. An airplane freighter might possibly be making a rescue trip up to Great Whale River Post, where a summer party of geologists had been stranded. Many men and a lot of ore samples must be brought out.

It would have to be a freighter! A big fellow this time! One that could carry everthing we needed! Once more Doutt and I listened to talk of a plane, this time with outward calm but with secret excitement. This time a freighter!

The story of the geologists, however, gave us some pause. They had been on a boat, and shipping time was

36

August. Yet not until now, the middle of January, had anyone been able to reach Moose Factory with the news. They had been literally marooned for five whole months at Great Whale River. One geologist with one Indian driver had finally made the trip down on a dog sled. All the more reason, we thought, to dread the dog trip up there, the 30 days of tight cheeks and numb noses, the 30 nights of dreaming about the days. In a plane we could leave now, lolling back in cushions, and sleep tonight at the post at Great Whale River.

A pilot was rumoured to be in the village.

George was willing. He was even cheerful. But he was *not walking!* We got new warm clothes on while he hitched up the dog team. Then we all made speed. We pushed swiftly through the island forests, scrambled once more down the steep bank of the river and crossed, once again, to Moosonee.

As you face North, Moose Factory is the end of civilization, but as you return, it is the beginning, and I think that while Mrs. Cargill lives there Moose Factory will be a white man's land; for the house at Moose Factory is a woman's house, with fine china and tall candles on the dinner table, a grand piano in the living-room (with a fringed Spanish shawl hanging rakishly from its top), and the bedroom is fitted with a matched set of furniture that might well have come from Grand Rapids. A few concessions to the north must be made, but within the house they are insignificant. The servant girl is an Indian; the bathroom is a washstand with a basin of icy water on it; the toilet is a tin chamber-pot inside a little wooden cupboard. And both upstairs and down, thick frost covers the window-panes. I slept in my underwear and refused to wash my face at all.

It was 41 below zero that first morning as we break-fasted, amused at three little black-capped chickadees that had flown in from the forest, awkward and unbalanced because their tails were all bent into a curve. The cold of last night, I suspected, had driven them into the cramping summer nest of a woodpecker — a fine shelter indeed if you have the dimensions. The chickadees had made it, but they were paying the price. Perhaps all day they would feel as awkward as puppies and puzzle about it as they pecked among the willow twigs.

Doutt and I went at once after breakfast to get the answer to our petition about the freighter, and for a little while after we got it, nothing could have made us complain. A freighter *would* go. And *we* could go with it! Our whole first month of toil was already over!

It was due Sunday or Monday, and would leave then for Great Whale River in the first lull of the wind. More time at our base! More time in the interior! We plunged into new fevers of calculation, for now new food stores must go along with us. We sat all morning with pencil and paper while Cargill, in disinterested fashion, advised us to carry in all but the commonest staples, such as flour and—well, flour. He sold us bacon, fruit, powdered milk, cheese and butter while we computed rations at three pounds per day for each man, and groaned at the weight of it.

We repacked next day and finished by sunset. From that minute on, we longed to go. We relaxed that night with the Indians' physician, the Scottish Doctor Tyrer, his wife and little daughter, sitting late at a big table in the living-room, listening to tales of the doctor's visits to the natives of Great Whale River, talking of the Indians with their seal-grease-and-flour (a common dietary mixture), of Epsom salts and tuberculosis, of inbreeding and the Arctic throat infection (of cause unknown, and much dreaded through the North). The doctor was neither sad nor hopeful about the future of the region. In winter, except near Moose Factory, he can do nothing. In summer there is no time to go inland. Sick natives must get to the post-house before August and wait until the little boat brings him.

Two more days went by, while we waited impatiently.

38

But hours here mean nothing. You speed away in your mind, accomplishing miracles, and come back reluctantly to watch snow falling, soft, thick and slow. You feel tough, but three miles in the cold leaves you burning all over. Your throat tissues are raw; your thighs great lumps of soreness from the outward swing of your legs (which keeps snowshoes from hitting together). You wonder anxiously what has happened to your "wind." At last, while you pretend to watch the snow-smoke whipping on a distant hill, you make yourself face the facts. You are soft all over, and you are more than halfway afraid. It doesn't shame you. You are simply flabbergasted.

It sounds like a slow transition, but a few hours can do it. From a man full of courage and great nonchalance, you become like a chickadee bewildered by new curves. But that stage swiftly passes, and soberly you begin to work through your crisis.

Simple confidence was not going to be enough. It.must be replaced with something more positive. The muscles must be more hardened, carefully, with gradual exercise. The mind must learn patience, if only for the conservation of nervous energy. In this country one would never be able to "take it or leave it." Obviously, one would take it! And one must become like little Catherine Tyrer, the doctor's child of only seven, who begged so hard to go up to Great Whale River—"Please, Daddy! And come back all by myself on the plane!" That was the spirit! That was positive! You must jump up and down with your yellow braids bouncing, and *beg* to take it!

On Wednesday, heavy wind and snow gave a bleak forecast when we waked, but by lunch the snow ceased, the wind died and the sun gleamed in almost cheerful fashion. The afternoon air was clear and between twenty and 25 below zero. In this relative warmth, Doutt and I went for snowshoe practice up to the north end of the island. There the *Churchill* was beached for the winter. Snow-blown, lonely, drifts banking the masts eerily and great wind-scooped hollows dug from the white tumbles beneath the hull, she stood in wooden racks bleakly waiting. This was a chapter in the life of the supply boat I had given no thought to. Yet for a Hudson Bay boat it is a long chapter. Four months in water! Eight months on land!

A ladder hung over her side, and Doutt and I, gratefully removing our snowshoes, climbed aboard, finding a cheerful carpenter taking time from repair work to warm himself in the heated cabin. We sat with him while he finished a smoke, and he and I "gaffed" about our west-coast acquaintances. Day passed swiftly. The sun failed in its promise. As we left the scene, we looked back at the death-like fantasy of the great icebound boat, with the groves of spruces in the foreground. The snowy river lay behind it in a wasteland, and even the sky seemed frozen.

That evening, ten or twelve guests—all the post employees as well as the Canadian Mountie and Doctor Tyrer—sat quietly in the Cargills' living-room, listening to the KDKA weekly broadcast of messages to men in the North. Bill Beal in Pittsburgh was speaking, relaying word to Northern men from their friends. Light from the oil lamp cast heavy shadows whenever anyone moved, shadows flowing along the walls and the floor in rich and harmonious pictures. But the listeners moved little. Their attitude was intent, almost reverent. This famous broadcast is the closest touch that Northern exiles can have with home. Many have not been outside for years. The long afternoon's exercise, the hot fire, the peaceful evening, made me wonderfully sleepy. When the broadcast ended, well after midnight, I could scarcely wait to say goodnight before I fell into bed.

On Thursday, we walked to Moosonee with letters for the first chance plane to Senneterre. There they would be mailed. The forest was a fairyland of queer-shaped stumps and snow-sagging branches. A spruce forest has a warmth about it, surprising and welcome. Shut in from the blast, one can wander there for hours. The fresh

40

snow, bewilderingly clean, reveals any track for some distance. We trailed a rabbit back under a snow-canopied bush and found his last night's bed. Beyond the bed lay the tracks of a weasel, and in the deep kick-back of snow and the length of the leap, we could read great speed in the escape of the rabbit. The weasel had next stopped at a bear-mouse hole. There his tracks disappeared, reappearing beyond, again were gone and again appeared. On this second hunt, the weasel had been digging along for hopeful stretches completely under the snow.

Friday was warm, only six below zero, with absolutely no wind. The sun shone brightly. We had begun to expect word from the plane, but Mr. Funk, in Moosonee, had none. Late in the afternoon, I wandered alone up and down the countless trails of the island in a labyrinth of white-draped spruces with whole banks of snow occasionally slipping from the down-pulled branches in one great mass. The snow, still mostly dry, fell in clouds, with very little "plop." Near dusk there was no longer any sliding snow, and I walked in what seemed more than a total silence. The sun lowered, and the snow floor of the forests gradually brightened, standing out sharply against the sombre green of the conifers. Once, the silence was suddenly broken by the clang of the mission bell, seemingly speaking to a very wide audience, for, like an answerer, a team of Husky dogs with wolfish abandon howled in unison and were themselves answered by howls from every direction of the settlement.

I stayed in the forest to watch blue shadows lengthen and the sun, as dull and yellow as corn, slip down into the southwestern horizon. I meant constantly to go home, but still lingered. Darkness came. Still I waited, while the moon rose bright and clear, and at intervals a Husky dog howled weirdly. Among the trees, the moon shadows shifted rapidly, alive and fanciful, following the moon's swift progress. I was cold indeed when I finally reached home.

How strange it seemed to be housed again! How wonderfully merry! We ate a hearty late supper and then sat all together about the heat of the stove, taking our unearned ease in the factor's cheerful living-room. What a potent medicine, peace! Already the work we had to do seemed less difficult, and nothing at all, now, seemed dull. By and by Mrs. Cargill at the piano began to play soft Scottish airs. Eventually she livened to martial music. This indeed was contentment.

The whole of Saturday remained cloudless, windless, crisp, a typical Northern day of its kind—although its kind in the North is not very common. A sunny day in sub-Arctic winter, perhaps because of its rarity, brings a picnic spirit, a universal feeling of gratitude. The Indian boys hauling wood for the numerous fires (they refuse to do much on Sunday) responded like starved plants to the sun, laughing and calling to each other. Distantly across the river, three Indians with a team hastened by, carrying back home what food and luxuries from the post-store they could transport and afford. Their dogs had an eager bark and the men moved at a quick pace. They laughed and gestured and seemed happy. There were only two dogs pulling; a man was hitched with them on a third line.

Our last night (supposedly) was the proper time for our guide, George, to make official farewells. When we next saw him, he was busily arranging a dance for himself, as was the local custom—a loud and boisterous square dance, with as many people as possible, so that he could wish himself well and start off exhausted, but at peace with tradition and all his friends.

On Sunday, the morning of mornings, the weather looked decidedly uncertain. The sun shone brightly, but there was a mackerel sky, a ring around the sun, and two sun-dogs. We saw these ominous signs with sorrow. There was hope, however, that if the plane came in early, as had been promised, it might leave at once, making Great Whale River on the same day and beating the storm. We were depressed when by noon the plane hadn't shown up, but at three-thirty someone saw it landing over Moosonee. In a rush we got out the tractor, loading food supplies and all baggage onto the sleigh.

Our pilot was Lymburner, famed Arctic pilot. He had a freighting ship, a Fairchild, splendid for Northern travel and the only plane of its type in the whole eastern Arctic. He told us that in this ship he had once carried two oxen, one at a time, in an especially arranged compartment. The oxen had weighed over a thousand pounds apiece. He could have handled all of our equipment, but since he was instructed to make two trips for the geologists, he preferred to leave our extra food for transport on his second trip. It demonstrates the faith with which Lymburner inspires people that my companion and I accepted this gamble without a murmur.

Back at the post, we were full of joy for tomorrow. The Cargills gave us a turkey dinner with fine food on the table and fine people around it. Just like Christmas all over again! In the evening more people came, even adventurous little Catherine Tyrer. I hated to leave the merry party while it was still young, but we had to be ready for an early take-off in the morning. It was not yet midnight when we said our goodbyes and left Moose Factory behind us, walking over to the hotel at Moosonee, through the forest along paths now grown familiar, across the little island so full of friendliness and quiet, half-regretting that it was for the last time. The moon shone brightly. In the silvery light, the trees, snowladen, seemed simply not real at all.

WINGS TO GREAT WHALE RIVER

"Bush" is the land of coniferous forests. "Barrens" or "tundra" is all the mossy and rocky Northland beyond the trees. Between the two lies central Ungava, the great transition, still mostly treeland, but with trees seldom worthy of the name. Our own movement would exactly parallel Nature's gradual movement from the "bush" to "true tundra"—from Moose Factory (where pines, spruces and aspens reach heights of 50 feet) to the Belcher Islands, an actual "land of the little sticks."*

In summer, on the once-a-year freighter, a traveller going north from Moose Factory and slowly leaving bush country sees the forests interspersed with grey-green tundra meadows on the slopes and heights of the higher hills; as he moves northward, the trees are more and more scattered. The immediate shore of the Bay, however, is always treeless, and is dismal grey with boulders. Rocks are strewn helter-skelter over the slow-rising coasts of all the central land. At river mouths and creek entrances, thick stands of willows are four to six feet high, dense drab mats of bushes with slender branches and long narrow leaves—for it is not so much cold as it is wind and moisture that matters to growing things, and wherever there is moisture and protection, the Ungava land gives forth growth in abundance. In every wind-free depression, in every protected valley, tamaracks and black spruces, even far into the interior, grow freely and green, pushing up the sheltered slopes and sometimes braving the very blasts themselves, as we were to see eventually, with a picturesque half-success.

I kept a few notes as we flew along in the plane:

I get an impression of the vastness of the country now such as I could get in no other possible way. Since I have seen it always before at close range, this short trip by plane is in every way good. George is really impressed! Every few minutes he looks down to check our location. About every quarter of an hour he announces excitedly that we have just finished another day's journey by dog sled. I am lazy enough at the moment to prefer it this way.

*A literal translation of the ancient Russian word "tundra."

44

At Fort George a woman ran out of her shack and waved her apron up at us. Before that, at Rupert's House, a woman opened the door of her house and stood staring up, shading her eyes.

To the west we have a dramatic spread of the Bay ice, which we are flying over now most of the time. This wide strip of ice extends into the water for a width of 20 to 30 miles. The edge is distinctly visible. It is wildly jagged and irregular in outline. We can trace deep leads (open cracks) beginning at the outer edge and running back in some places almost to the shore. "Rough ice" seems from here to have definite and repeated form, to lie speckled in lilypad formations — a freakish beauty. At the far edge of the ice huge blocks are piled up in the usual pressure ridges. They are also high at many places along the shore. At every jut of land are the great barriers of pressure ice, and huge blocks loom up in the main ice bed, here and there. But we do not spend much time or attention on the ice strip, for beyond it, seeming near despite the twenty miles of distance, stretches the black open water of the Bay.

From the west-side windows a moment ago, I noticed a little cloudiness. The big white fog banks are now moving in upon us. It is an omniscient sort of feeling, being here, watching them slowly form. They are soft and fleecy at first. But already they are beginning to drift in masses about the plane. Just now we dove right through a little one, swimming for a few moment in pure nothingness. Now we are in the clear again. When we are in the midst of them, these clouds are no longer white, but are grey-coloured. I think we are in for a real fog battle. They are beginning to pile up on us. Almost constantly we are flying into them, and we are taking longer and longer to come out of it.

The pilot tried to climb above the bank. We went to

45

3000 feet without finding any thinning out whatever. We then went very low, trying to fly beneath it, but the air remained the same. We had to plough ahead, fog or no fog. We had had a bad half-hour before suddenly the air seemed to be thinning out a little. More light came into the plane from outside. We strained to see, and could again make out the dark line of open Bay water. Suddenly, in a single instant, we broke into bright sunshine. We had apparently flown through a last thick cloud and now had left the whole fog completely behind.

A flock of ptarmigan just flew up from behind a hill and dove in behind some rocks a little way off. This is a new angle for bird observations. Being all white against whiteness, the birds were like movement without body—or possibly a flurry of snowflakes, rising up and falling below us. I am getting terribly sleepy. . . .

About four in the afternoon, we spotted the little house. "That's it!" cried George, pointing excitedly. The mechanic jerked his thumb down in the direction of the Great Whale River Post. It was like a toy lost in the snow, a tiny box of red and white. "It would have been a month with dogs," George was saying, in an awed voice.

The plane made a big swing around the back of the post-house as Lymburner headed it into the gentle west wind and landed on the frozen river. The flying box-car rested and the mechanic unfastened the door. We bolted out. We stood on the river ice and stared upward at the little house. It was on the edge of the cliff-like river bank, and somebody was boisterously waving his arms from the top of the path that pitched and twisted down the long slope toward us. Three men were starting down the path, pulling on mittens as they came. The path was steep and glistening, hardpacked with much trampling of feet. The North is always a friendly place, but these men had a fiercer friendliness, compounded of relief and great joy.

"Boy! You're really anxious," said the mechanic to the first man who reached us. He grinned.

"My name's Jack," he said warmly as we all shook hands. "I'm one of the geologists. We sure are glad to see you!"

"How long have you been stuck here?" asked Doutt, to check up on the rumours, and Jack said that ever since September they had been waiting to get word through to the south. Their boat had broken up just before the freeze and not until now had it been considered safe for the dog team to start out over the snows from Great Whale River. The white man who had come into Moosonee was one of the geologists, and the dogs and the Indian driver belonged to the Great Whale River Post.

Roy Jeffries, who looked not older than seventeen, next introduced himself as the apprentice to the Great Whale River factor, while the factor himself was slowly descending the steep, slippery path with a gentlemanly caution, in a beautiful cream-and-brown caribou parka. His name was Norman Ross, and in the thick caribou hide he looked as big as two men. (Caribou hair is about two inches long, very soft and very wavy.) Norman Ross had a formal, unhurried way, very impersonal in contrast to the eager greetings of the others. He watched the scene thoughtfully for a little while before he returned to the house, looking Englishman and gentleman to the core.

Roy Jeffries was staring into the plane compartment where our fifteen big packing-cases—each a load for a burro—as many duffle-bags, a dozen wooden food boxes, a gunny sack of bacon slabs, cameras, tripods, mechanical equipment too various to describe all waited to be unpacked.

"Why didn't you bring something with you?" Roy asked, grinning.

"You'll need it all," said a geologist sagely, slapping his mittened hands together in the cold. "I hope it's to eat!" They crowded to have a look.

47

"Some of it is," we admitted.

"Let's dish it out," decided Roy, and the two of us climbed inside. We were pretty warm inside the plane, for handling that heavy stuff is not easy, and we made a silly competition of it to show off speed and muscles. The rest received the stuff, crawling off with it like burdened ants up the steep path. We could see them tugging and climbing whenever we glanced through the window of the plane. Roy had on a black jumbo sweater and sealskin boots, and seemed scarcely more than a boy. But he was strong and more than willing.

"Chop a hole in this thing," he cried out once to the mechanic as we kept bumping our heads on the close, domed ceiling above us. "My back's got knots in it."

"Some of these are for Ross," I explained, as we finished the wooden boxes.

"Food," commented Roy. "We're down to a few potatoes. Boy! This is getting to be a regular metropolis."

"You like company, don't you?" I asked him, curious. "It's better than being alone, isn't it?"

Roy thought it over. "For me, yes," he decided. "But not for all the men up here. Some of the men get used to being alone. They don't like it, but they don't want to be bothered much either."

"I can see how they might feel that way," I said. Eventually we finished and yelled up to the men above us not to come back down.

"How about a cup of coffee?" Roy suggested. "That would be good idea!" (Roy, I soon learned, was always concluding that coffee would be a good idea.)

"I want to see them anchor it," I explained as we stepped out of the plane (although the air was freezing me). "You go on up." But of course he wouldn't.

We had already seen the mechanic lugging drained oil from the engine up the steep path to the house, carrying it in an old black pail. The oil would have to be heated in the kitchen before the plane started again in the morning.

The nose of the machine stood raised ten or twelve feet

and the canvas hood had been thrown over it, the flaps hanging on either side clear to the ground, tenting the engine completely. The hood was tightly laced from underneath to keep out blowing, finely sifted snow.

At the end of either wing were two iron handles. Ropes were run through these, each rope tied to the middle of a long stick. The mechanic chopped out a narrow trench in the river ice, the length of each stick, and then buried the sticks in the trenches, lying flat.

Several bedraggled Indians in dirty old canvas parkas stood at a little distance silently smiling at the dogs, who were creeping up stealthily, sniffing the plane, and immediately bolting away. They were scrubby-looking dogs, perhaps belonging to the Indians, although Indians do not often use dogs.

"Pail!" yelled the mechanic, looking about for it. It was given to him, filled from the nearby water hole. The mechanic poured the water into the trenches and submerged the anchor sticks for a couple of inches. In just a few moments the water would be frozen solid. Being now in windy Ungava, Lymburner insisted on two anchors to each side of the plane.

"How about coffee?" cried Roy again, as I started up the path ahead of him. "Beat it!" he added, less polite now that we knew each other better, and pressing impatiently at my heels. Apparently we were to be "just boys" together. We made a race for it, climbing as fast as we could go. I was winded when I reached the top, but comforted that the boyish Roy was too!

"That's steep," I managed to say, panting.

"Steep!" cried Roy, in a delirium of sociability, "you tell 'em!"

The path led around the house to the door at the back. The front door was deeply snowdrifted, never used at all. We entered through the leanto, the shed always provided by the kitchen door for the natives to rest in. We went through the kitchen, assaulted by coffee odours and the cozy sound of men's voices. Two Indian women in long

49

black Government coats, like two old crows, sat on the floor in the unheated shed, staring and giggling as we passed through. In the warm kitchen, lighted by a dim yellow-gleaming kerosene lamp, Mary Took-a-Look, as Roy introduced her, was fussing with dishes. As we shook hands, she giggled excitedly in the seemingly silly native way, and almost literally stuck her head in the corner. But that was only a gesture for strangers. I knew that tomorrow all would be different.

Mary Took-a-Look was the regular Eskimo post-cook, but the geologists' own cook, a middle-aged Swedish fellow, wordless and efficient, was actually getting the supper at the stove. I judged that Mary had been having a cooking vacation since the coming of the geologists. Roy poured out my coffee and got some for himself.

"Hungry?" he said as we carried our drinks into the other room.

"I could go for anything," I admitted.

"Well, we still have a few potatoes," said Ross sharply, overhearing us. There was a sudden hush throughout the room at this and appreciative glances passed from one to the other of the men. "Of course, your stuff," said Ross, with a twinkle in his eyes, "is still out in the warehouse. We didn't break into that!"

We clustered like bees around the stove, warming. The men wanted news. What did people think outside? Did they think that the geology party was lost? We told them that some of the newspapers had reported them ship-wrecked, but the messenger to Moose Factory must have ended that story already. As we talked, Mary Took-a-Look was spreading over the bare table a heavy white cotton tablecloth. Among the men, she was sullen and defensive. Perhaps four new boarders broke the camel's back, after the six or seven who had already stayed for five months! The brilliant white-lighted Aladdin lamp suspended above the table was strangely pretty with its delicate, moth-like mantle and the spirit and fullness of its glow.

"Does it look like home?" I asked Doutt presently, for he had been there in the summer.

"Yes," said Doutt, pleased. "I still like it."

We had strawberry jam for supper (HBC brand, and good), homemade bread in big crusty slices piled high on a round plate, canned bully-beef, raisin pie and coffee.

"Where does all this come from?" I asked Ross.

"It's in honour of the new supplies," said Ross cheerfully.

"And this?" I added, tapping my water glass, while he explained that Boyshish, the Indian boy, hauled it up the steep bank every morning from the river and brought it to the house. He carried two pails at a time on a wooden yoke that lay across his shoulders.

"Just like a Chinaman," Ross added lazily. "Every morning he fills up that big barrel in the kitchen."

The Swedish cook had set everything out on the table and gone back to the cookstove to eat his own supper. He was a heavy man, but he moved, in soft-soled sealskin shoes, with scarcely a sound. I sat there thinking that Great Whale River might be a "metropolis" just now, but it was still a thousand miles from a city and a month by dog team from the nearest train.

"Pretty good floors you have here," I told Ross. "No squeaking."

For the first time Ross gave me his really serious attention. "When the temperature goes very low," he admitted, "they really do squeak. But they're good floors, nevertheless." Then the men kidded him about spending all his time polishing them. "I like to keep the place up," Ross defended himself with boyish satisfaction.

"Ross is just a homebody," commented one of the geologists.

I noticed the easy-chair, the radio and the bookcase surmounted by a huge dictionary, but what took my eye was an old upright piano! The tale of the piano was a complicated story which Ross promised to tell me later. "It used to be Flaherty's," he volunteered briefly, sending

51

a thrill up my spine. When I looked again it had an aura about it. "It used to be Flaherty's!"

Lymburner was the actual centre of attention that evening. The men hung on his words. Once or twice the Swedish fellow brought the big white enamelled pot to refill the coffee-cups. Once Mary Took-a-Look brought in an extra pitcher of Klim (powdered milk mixed with water). After supper we pushed our chairs back and teetered while Lymburner obligingly talked. Ross sat at one end of the table and Roy Jeffries at the other. There was little in this post-house to be compared with Moose Factory. Great Whale River was completely a man's world. Almost everyone had questions for Lymburner, about the Antarctic, penguins and the girls at Rio. With Doutt and me he discussed cameras and lenses. He had used an 8 mm. camera in the Antarctic. We had to use 16 mm. to make pictures large enough for popular projection. He knew what we were up against in the ice and snow.

"But what about the girls at Rio?" insisted some of the men, hoping for a luscious story.

"Smart girls," said Lymburner soberly. "Know a lot of languages! I went to a café once with an international assortment of men—Spanish, Norwegian, French, English and German. A girl stopped at our table and talked with each of us in his own language!"

"So what?" the men insisted impatiently.

"So we gave her a meal," concluded Lymburner, laughing, and would not go into the subject further.

We questioned the geologists hopefully about inland conditions, but they, like everyone else, knew the interior only from a boat in summer.

"You never saw worse wind," said Jack. "You'd never get me in there in the wintertime."

Even in September, three of the boys had been blown out to sea in a small boat, driven through the Gulf Hazard and out of Richmond Gulf. But their boat had hit a small island, where they had lived for three days without food.

"One of us was so scared before we hit the island that he really thought that he was already dead. He was all curled up on the bottom of the boat, and even after it landed, he wouldn't move until the wind had all died down."

But they wouldn't say which man it was.

"We built a rock shelter on the island to lie in; just a little circular wall to keep us out of the blast."

"There are more men in this room tonight," said Ross, half wonderingly, near bedtime, "than will be in it probably for the next ten years!"

The first view of the house had been deceptive. There were two bedrooms on the second floor. Jack had already been sleeping up there. Ross' and Jeffries' rooms were just across the hall from the living-room downstairs. Lymburner slept on the living-room couch in a sleeping-bag that he always carried, and the mechanic, poor fellow, slept beside him on the floor. I suppose they were used to it. Mary Took-a-Look probably went to some native *tupek*.[3] The Swedish cook slept in the cubbyhole "office" that opened directly from the kitchen. The majority of the men went out-of-doors at bedtime. Ross stopped Jack and Roy as they started off.

"Show these fellows the lay of the land," he said, waving toward Doutt and me. The four of us went upstairs together.

Doutt and I shared a room, rolling out our sleeping-bags on two bare, narrow cots in an otherwise unfurnished chamber. We heard the men calling to each other outside as they plodded over the snow to their beds at the warehouse. Ross and Lymburner talked below us for a few minutes in low, night-time voices, and then all was quiet. At last we were at Great Whale River, I remember thinking just before we slept, but my conscience was hurting a little as I remembered how Jeff and I had kidded the geologists.

"Pretty apt to be a blizzard in the morning," Jeff had said to me, with a wink. "And if it lasts three days, as it

53

probably will, it may go on to six."

"Over on the west coast," I had agreed circumstan-
tially, "one of those six-day blizzards this time of year
runs on to about eighteen. It's almost a proverb at
Churchill."

They had laughed, but we hadn't been funny. How
anxious they were to get out! And how happy we were to
be in!

"Is it really this way all the time over here on the east
coast?" I asked Jeff at the next opportunity. "No guffaws?
No beating the dogs up? No noisy business? I haven't
heard a cuss-word since I heard it in French!"

Jeff looked at me for a minute, puzzled, as if he didn't
know what I was saying, and then he came to with a
laugh.

"Oh! Cussin'? Nope. This is just the way it is!" (But he
went on thinking.) "What the heck is the use of cussin',"
he asked me finally, "when there ain't no-one around to
hear it?"

A faint stink of oil invaded the bedrooms the next
morning and reminded me that this was the day. I heard
the kitchen door shut heavily and the increased volume
of voices below.

"It's a good day," announced Lymburner. "We're
gonna go. Right now. No time to lose." He had a loud but
unexcited voice, and always spoke very briskly but
unhurried. I heard the scraping of chairs as I hastened to
dress. The others were making room for Lymburner's
chair at the breakfast table.

From the kitchen door I saw the large enclosed oil tin
standing on the back of the black iron range. It looked like
an old dark miniature barrel. The oil smell was a positive
stench. Mary Took-a-Look was washing the dishes, with
one of the geologists on guard where the oil was heating.
He saluted me silently, with a cheery lift of his hand, and
turned back to his patient watching. No-one spoke when
I entered the living-room. They merely made room for

my chair and handed down the oatmeal that had gone begging. They were finishing, but I soon caught up, and we had a last round of coffee all together. Through the half-cleaned window I could see the sky, clear, if not sunny, and the men commented on the way the sides of the plane reflected light from the snow and sparkled like silver. Murray Franke, the head of the expedition, was giving my friend Jack last-minute instructions about the ore samples that would not be carried until the second trip.

"Aren't you going today?" I asked Jack.

"Nope," Jack said, all too carelessly. "I've been waiting here since last summer. I guess I can stand it for another day or two." This really called for a crack, but nobody made it. The geologists had always seemed to me to have a general air of depression, a numbness, I suppose, natural to their long state of resignation. Since they did not seem willing to talk about their work (or perhaps were not allowed to), conversation was difficult.

When the mechanic came into the kitchen for the oil, the other men began to grab everything together. The mechanic picked up the pail, warm and heavy, and slowly started down the long, slippery hill. Ross did not bother to go down. Slumped comfortably in his chair, his feet in soft, old brown leather house slippers, he was in no mood to get cold, and said so, pulling gently on his after-breakfast cigarette.

"I know one thing," said somebody, breaking the general silence, "I'll be glad to get some honest-to-God tobacco!" They had all been smoking the vile "cut plug," beloved of the Eskimos.

Someone asked about the Swede. "Oh, he's down at the other shack, getting ready to leave."

"I wouldn't want to lose him," said someone else.

"Oh, I'll take him," put in Ross. A few of them laughed. They were not scintillating. The geologists all had something that they were brooding over. The past? The future? Who could say?

The crowd was close on the heels of the mechanic as he made his descent. The plane had a fire-pot directly under the engine, and as we went down the cliff, we could hear the roaring burner. It stood on a platform under the canvas flaps of the hood that held heat around the engine, and the mechanic kept sticking his head through a slit in the canvas to make sure that everything was all right. There was, no doubt, some danger of fire; it is a chance flyers take in such country.

The mechanic climbed onto the top of the engine, while one of the men handed up the oil. The burner still roared. Crouched cautiously beside his oil can, the mechanic pulled the top of the hood back and let the oil travel down through a long tube. Then Lymburner stopped the noise, brought the heater out from under the tent flaps, and the mechanic dropped the hood to the ground and climbed down after it immediately; lastly, he folded the canvas and stored it in the plane. Franke didn't need to count noses. His men were all there.

They showed a little interest when I wanted to take a picture. I took two, which was all that the cold would allow before my camera shutter would begin to freeze up. I got one motion-picture shot of the plane in colour, for half the beauty of the thing was its delicate red and blue lettering against the silver body within the white world of snow. But two feet of film were all that I could get. My movie shutter had frozen tight and I could never again take motion pictures until spring came, when we expected to be out of Ungava. (Throughout the winter, I wore my "still" camera on a strap around my neck under my parka, and in coldest weather pushed it for added insurance into my armpit, and always kept it with me in my sleeping-bag while on the trail at night.)

As the mechanic dropped the hood, Lymburner mounted and slid shut the partition to the cockpit.

"Time to go!" yelled the mechanic, but he really needn't have said anything. In spirit the men were already started, if not already at home. They waited in a cluster at the plane door, like bees at the swarm, huddled against each other in coldness and impatience, doubtless still in dread lest something should prevent the take-off.

I could see Lymburner's head bent over the controls. We heard the starter in a mounting whine, like a turbine, and then the shriek as it took hold. The propeller started to move. It was slow at first, increasing in speed until Lymburner opened the throttle wide and all became one great blur of sound.

It was the "full-gun," to test her out. There was such a roar that we could hear nothing else. An Eskimo pup had been snooping at the rear of the plane. The cloud of snow and the rush of wind from the propeller drove suddenly full upon him, blasting his fur almost inside out. He was swept from his feet and sent spinning across the slippery river. Roy Jeffries was right beside me. I could see him bent almost double with laughing, but I couldn't hear him. Several times Lymburner opened the throttle and then the engine idled for a few moments, neatly chucking and swishing.

"Okay" Lymburner cried finally, sticking his head out of the cockpit window. "Ready to go!"

The men climbed in feverishly now, and the mechanic climbed after them, shutting the door. Lymburner turned to us, waved his hand, slid his window shut and gunned the motor. The plane slowly taxied out over the river-snow. The big two-foot skis, twelve or fourteen feet long, had polished oak runners, golden-coloured when they caught the light. The plane rode like a magical sled for about three-eighths of a mile and then gracefully took the air. It circled back over us and headed straight south. Lymburner waved again as they passed by. We all stood lost in that kind of wonder that men always feel before the miracle of an airplane and in the admiration that they have for the "bag-o'-bones."*

"Weather permitting," he had said the night before,

*Northern white men's term for any pilot of a plane.

"we will leave in the morning." It was a cheerful, non-committal platitude, but it seemed to describe the very character of the man.

The first to move from the spot was the geologist Jack, of whom I had been, up to now, unaware. He was starting ahead of us before I got a good look at him.

"Got work to do," he said.

"We've got work to do, too," cried Doutt energetically, for he bore the official responsibility for the inland expedition in which I was only an assistant.

"Can't begin too soon," I said. Now that I had time to look around and take a lonely breath, my pulse beat faster. It was a big job, but we were gaining on it. It was only 15 January, and we were already at Great Whale River — two weeks ahead of schedule. Ross would need time to get hold of Kooke, the Eskimo whom Doutt had arranged with two summers ago to guide our party in. In the meantime, we must check over our stored summer shipment, pack all our supplies into sled-loads, get all advance information possible on the probable conditions of the interior, prepare our Belcher Islands equipment and leave it ready for the sled ride across the ice bridge to Tukarak.

"I suppose Ross ought to be allowed to recover from the geologists," I suggested to Doutt, but we both decided that Ross would just have to bear it.

"How about the invoices?" Doutt asked Ross as we all gathered again in the cozy living-room. "The sooner we get busy, the sooner you'll get rid of us!"

"All right," said Ross wearily, but apparently not unwilling. "I'll get my boots on and take you down to the storehouse—this afternoon."

In the old warehouse was soft light and silence, the kind of light and silence described by Thomas Hardy when he says that some barns seem to him like churches. The warehouse was enormous, the foundations perhaps 50 by 75 feet.[4] It dwarfed all the other post buildings. Inside, with the ceiling low and the windows small and high, light entered from both east and west, strongly emphasizing the heavy beams, thick old brown rafters that I reached up and examined curiously with my hand. An ancient flintlock rested there on two nails beside a modern .303 British, both rusted past usefulness. Another old gun, a 30-30 Winchester, hung at the north end of the room. Against the far north wall brown piles of full gunny sacks reached to the ceiling, and there too stood stores of sacked flour, sugar and oatmeal. One gunny sack, which was split open, revealed the gunny to be protective only, covering many other small white sacks. Most flour sacks were very light 25-pound packages, put up, of course, so that the natives could carry them in a kayak or on a toboggan.

"Here you are," said Ross at the south corner. "Here's your stuff, just as it came off the *Churchill.* I've got invoices that cover, but you check it over for yourselves."

There was our stuff. Flour sacks in the gunny. Bully-beef in that small box. Food in the fifteen or twenty large wooden boxes, and in the smaller ones our ammunition. And there lay three two-foot lengths of black tin stovepipe (I had a momentary chill from the coming nights as I saw them). All were neatly piled. Ross was neat about everything.

Ross led on, up a plank unskirted stairway with a raw board for the hand rail and the wooden steps much hollowed, for the warehouse was very old. From rafters above our heads as we climbed hung many fox traps, smooth-jawed, but red with rust.

"This wet air," said Ross, "is pretty hard on everything." Glancing down at the first floor, I noticed the sifting white below one of the flour sacks where a mouse must have been at work. Our moccasined feet had made no noise as we prowled about, the stairs quietly squeaking out the only sound, very small in that silence.

The upper room, with deeper windows and with pointed ceiling, seemed spacious by comparison. Fine fox skins, eight or ten to the bunch, were tied together through the mouths and slung over the free beams, heads uppermost, bushy tails hanging down. Red foxes brightened the line. Luscious cross-foxes showed dark fur gleaming and white tips dotting the tails. There were one or two bunches of fine snowy Arctic foxes and a few skins of silver. Five-foot wooden harpoon shafts for hunting walruses stood grouped in a corner and a few rested on rusty nails along the walls. Four wooden boxes full of dark clothing stood open, the distribution of the Government for destitute Indians (given out only at Ross' judgment), and at the far end of the room some rough-hewn bookcases held prayer books, hymnals and Bibles— the Anglican mission supplies. I picked up a Bible to examine the dots and triangles that make up the weird hieroglyphics of the Indian-Eskimo script, an alphabet given to the natives of the east shore by missionaries and the only written language of either the Indians or the Eskimos. A mass of tubes, strings and rusty metal pieces made a dirty heap beneath one window on the floor. Ross looked pained when I stopped to see it, and then he told me the promised story of the living-room piano.

It had been on *Laddie,* Flaherty's original boat. When he was leaving the Belchers, Flaherty, in gratitude and affection, made lavish presents, giving the natives as nearly as possible whatever they asked. To old Wetalltok, who so loved music, he had given the miraculous player-piano, but Wetalltok had been unable to do anything with it, and he had sledged it clear across the ice bridge to the Ungava mainland, expecting to sell it to the factor at the Great Whale River Post. But the factor had been transferred that fall to Fort George, 185 miles south of Great Whale River. Then poor old Wetalltok sledged the piano all the way down to Fort George, but was still unable to sell it.*

I was never able to learn just how or when the piano was brought up from Fort George. I believe it was finally transported by boat. For some years now it had stayed at Great Whale River. The manager before Ross had decided one winter to see what the player mechanism was composed of and had been unable to put the parts back together. It was the piano pieces that I now looked at on the floor of the warehouse. With them lay some cloth-topped overshoes and some moccasin-rubbers, dusty and unmated.

Ross left us to our own devices, and with hammer and wrecking bar two of us opened boxes while the other held the invoice list. We laid out the tea, dried fruit, canned goods, carefully saving the packings of excelsior, which we should need later for shipping specimens. Our eyes, accommodating themselves to the gradually changing

*A letter to Flaherty from Maver, the factor at Great Whale River, read: "Perhaps you will remember having given your pianola to Wetalltok just before you left the Belcher Islands last fall. Well, Wetalltok was stuck with that pianola on his hands; he couldn't take it into his igloo, and he couldn't live in your cabin, for he had, of course, no fuel. So he conceived the idea of sledging that pianola over to me—it seemed that you told him I would be keen to buy it—but how he could transport a full-size pianola over 85 miles of sea ice, and some of it rafted mighty high at that, was more than I could see, but he did it—brought it right into Great Whale Post, only to find that I wasn't there, for I had been transferred in the fall, south to Fort George. . . . So he kept on down the coast, having obtained supplies from the factor on the strength of the sale of the pianola to me, and after the Lord knows how many days, he came sledging in one day at nightfall, right into my post yard, with a "Chimo" and a "Here, Angarooka, is the box with the many insides." The thing worked, you'll be surprised to hear, though some of its notes were what Wetalltok called 'sick sounds'!" (Quoted from Robert J. Flaherty, *My Eskimo Friends: "Nanook of the North"* [Garden City, NY: Doubleday, Page & Co., 1924], p. 75.)

light, made us unaware of a bad storm raging, but suddenly, at about four o'clock, we could no longer see. We opened the door and full in our faces met the grounddrifter! Above the snow the sun was bright and the air was clear, as we later discovered, but the wind along the ground was blowing so wildly that the post-house was completely obliterated. Ice particles cut our faces sharply. The moist Ungava wind whipped us and chilled us through, even on a walk of so short a distance.

"Ungava wind!"—I remembered they used to tell me in the books. "From the iceberg-laden waters of the Davis Strait."

Probably it was George who found the path, being more used than we were to keeping his way while he travelled blind. But we seemed to have a consensus of feeling about the location of the house and got there after a bad five minutes.

"Come in, come in," called Ross, "and keep the wind out." Hastily we shut the door. I stopped in the kitchen to look at two dead birds about the size of pullets that lay in an immaculate whiteness of shining feathers upon the kitchen table. They were like fluffy snow. Except that blood had already dried on them, they would have been fine specimens.

"Where did these ptarmigan come from?" I asked Ross, and he said that a couple of natives had brought them in. These were willow ptarmigan, not the rock ptarmigan of the coast that I had expected. These had lived, no doubt, in the dense willow thickets along the many small streams that feed Great Whale River.

"I don't suppose there's much bird life in the interior?" I surmised.

"Dunno," said Ross. "I shouldn't think so."

"When can we get after our seal?" asked Doutt.

"Can't say that either," Ross continued. "I'll send a man out to find Kooke on Monday—that is, if the weather clears up by Monday." (Kooke was at his winter camp, a good day's journey up the coast.) Ross understood that we felt impatient, but he had learned patience with men as well as with the weather and was not too disgusted. "Just keep your shirt on," he would counsel sagely. "Everything will come about in due time."

Ross had a well-padded, comfortable armchair, and a favourite old smoking-jacket that he liked to wear in the evening. He was proud of his house. He had put lots of time on it.

"They furnish the material if we are willing to work," he said, speaking of the Hudson's Bay Company. "I built the upstairs rooms all by myself; I've even got a place up there for a bathroom, but of course there aren't any fixtures."

"Do you call that little place a bathroom?" asked Jack, who had just joined us.

"Yes, indeed," Ross declared proudly. "That's the way I keep up my courage."

"Well," said Jack, with admiration, "if you finally *take to the bush,* it won't be your fault."

"What about Old Harold?" I asked Jack, speaking of that well-known Swedish figure, the Indians' interpreter at Great Whale River. "Is he *bushed* yet?"

"Judge for yourself," advised Jack, smiling. "Go down and get him to tell you some stories."

"He been here 40 years," put in Ross. "If he's not bushed yet, then he never will be."

Even on the west coast I had heard of Old Harold. He was the captain of a Swedish boat, long ago, had been wrecked and stranded in his youth near Great Whale River, and there he had stayed. He had become an early factor for the Hudson's Bay Company, married an Eskimo woman, and now knew a great deal about the native languages. He had been an important instrument in Flaherty's "discovery" of the Belchers and Flaherty had freely acknowledged it.[5]

"Old Harold's the only one left who knows about the early days," Ross added. "You ought to see him."

"We ought to see you too," I told him, "and get you to

answer some questions."

"Better wait until after supper," said Ross, "then we can have a session."

Mary Took-a-Look was bringing the food in and setting it down in a highly executive manner, for now that the Swede was gone, she had come back into her own.

"Fancy," said Ross as we ate, "being in a sweat to start out for the Seal Lakes country!"

Jack shook his head in a depressed manner. "You can have it," he said sympathetically. "Listen to that wind. It will sure kill the broadcast," Jack ventured further, a little note that threw a shadow over everything. It was our last chance at a broadcast until spring came, as Ross had reminded us.

"You think you'll get a message from your wife?" asked Jack hopefully, and I felt a mounting glow in my head. In this lonely land the thought of word from Sally was very exciting. The broadcast was scheduled for midnight from Pittsburgh.

"Too bad," said Ross, unmoved, "that it couldn't be at some hour so that a man could get to bed."

Our promised session with Ross after dinner was dark and disturbing. It was soon obvious that the original arrangement should have been made with the Hudson's Bay Company and not with the Eskimo Kooke.

"It's wrong," said Ross of our fine plan, "from start to finish. Farther north you might do it, but not here. Eskimos rarely go into the bush, or into the interior at all. Not from this part of the coast they don't. This part of the interior is all Indians' land. Trees mean toboggans. Dogs and sled can't move through the loose snow in there. The surface never freezes all over. The temperature isn't constant. And the wind is the worst thing. Look at it!" He jerked his thumb toward the window. "Listen to it! Men who live in *that* have to know how! I wouldn't go into the interior with a *komatik* even if I *knew* I could come out of it!" For once Ross had been eloquent.

64

But we told ourselves, dismayed, no-one had really tried it! We planned to travel on the frozen waterways, taking to the trees only for wind shelter during a storm. On the map at least we could be guided in by Little Whale River.

"But you can't go in on Little Whale," Ross objected. "There must be something wrong with it! I never heard of an interior Indian who took any direction but straight up the coast to Richmond Gulf or just off into the bush. If Little Whale could be used, then the Indians would use it!"

In confused indecision we spent the rest of the evening still stubbornly computing rations, assuming that, if so advised by the Eskimo Kooke, we would still try to use sleds. Seven weeks might be necessary for the trip inland. Two teams—meaning sixteen dogs—would eat 1140 pounds of dog food. With only three helpers, we ourselves would eat 882 pounds. This allowed but three and a half pounds per man daily, which is really inadequate. We "died hard." We had greatly admired our little plan. Any lesser man than the patient Ross would have been hot under the collar that we didn't take advice more readily.

The wind howled and the drifter raged on; whirling masses of white swept the plain furiously and the walls of the house seemed charged with sound. I had seen snowstorms all my life in Alberta, but nothing like this one.

"It's packing down out there," Jack told us, "like concrete. But upstairs you might find everything clear. I'll bet the moon's shining into your bedroom window."

But we didn't go up to see. The living-room was too warm and too comfortable and I was too much depressed. "No use thinking any more tonight," Doutt and I finally decided. "I'll just wait now," I thought, "for my messages." Perhaps everything we did before midnight that evening was actually only to pass the time away. And then we couldn't hear the broadcast! The wind howled outside like a whole colony of loons. That static was

65

terrific. Sometimes we heard music, a little, or the sound of a voice, but mostly static. "Ground-drifter," was the simple verdict, but we all strained and listened for a long time, feeling that things would surely get better.

It was a last bitter disappointment on an evening of nothing but disappointment. We had stayed up late and were tired and despondent for nothing but faint sounds that could have been music.

Upstairs we looked from the window and saw that Jack was right. Ungava was a weird country. Above the whirling, blindingly blowing snowstorm, the sky way perfectly clear, the moon shone brightly, and even the stars were visible.

KOOKE THE CAKE-EATER

The waiting for Kooke was very much easier than the waiting that came after. Jack, the geologist, already acquainted with the country, took us for a walk on the seventeenth, the first day that the wind let up. We started out on snowshoes over open plains of hard snow, plains broken by scattered clumps of stunted spruce trees. No-one was in high spirits, for the ground-drifter here had meant a storm to the south and possible trouble for the plane.

The open slopes were packed hard—as always after a strong wet wind has hit them — and snowbanks had been blasted into fantastic swoops, juts and swirls that threw queer shadows. A light breeze still blew, but not enough to disturb the driven surface of this well-iced land. We headed for distant spruces where would be whatever birds or animals there were. The sun was perceptible but dull and low in the sky. The light reflected from the ground was disturbing but not painful. We assumed comfortable squints and concentrated on efficiency with the snowshoes, keeping to the edges of windswept hills as much as possible, since the hollows at their bases looked almost bottomless with drifts. No sharp lines remained. It was a dizzy world, a universal flowing of one vast curve into another. I had almost less a walking than a swimming sensation.

The trees in the spruce grove grew close together, small, twisted, hugging the ground. Trees grew naturally straight only in protected places. The first grove was a mile and a half from the post-house, and there I found my first birds. They would be ptarmigan, I knew, following the trail of the quaint winter "snowshoes"—for the ptarmigan is a highly adaptable bird and spreading flanges of growth appear in cold weather all around its feet, giving it natural snowshoes. The fresh tracks wandered from one thicket to another, and soon we found the night shelter (known as the "night-form"), a fresh hole dug from a snowbank, always the ptarmigan's refuge from darkness or storm. Eventually we found the birds themselves. Three of them sat snowy and motionless at the edge of the clearing.

Jack thought that we tricked him, denying the existence of any birds. He didn't know what to look for. There is a tiny black glint from a ptarmigan's eyes. These birds faced us, and were head down, feeding on a willow twig sticking up for a few inches through the snow. The ptarmigan were the identical tone of the whiteness around them and were almost literally invisible. They looked up quietly as we neared, and stopped feeding. We paused and waited. At last, as if bored, they began to walk toward another clump of willows, where they made a fine meal on the tips, and were half-finished before Jack acknowledged their being—with chagrin. Having fed, the three white birds sat quietly close together, waiting or resting, white, motionless and silent, staring out over the snow.

We pushed in among the spruces, for we heard the faint whispering of wings there, and at last the sudden sharp cry of a Canada jay broke over us. Some branches still trembled and were brushed free of snow, and below

67

them (for the hard-packed surface on this particular morning supported even the jay that never grows any snowshoes) stood the little grey-and-white mottled bird with the *very* long tail that had given the cry. He was alone, and for a startled moment eyed us intently before he cried again and bolted. All the Canada jays at Great Whale River were surprisingly wild and afraid.

For two more hours we searched the grove and the surrounding thickets, finding few signs of life. I examined the night shelters of the ptarmigan that dig into a drift for about six inches, never trying to turn around in their tunnels, but simply digging through the drift in the morning and out on the other side. The pile of black droppings that they always leave in a night-form makes it easy for anyone to find it. There seemed to be no animals at all just then in the vicinity of Great Whale River. We did not spy even a rabbit track.

We were headed home when we heard ahead of us the quick chattering of chickadees (Hudsonian chickadees). Six fluffy round balls in the pale winter hues of grey and brown flew back into a spruce tree, bounding from branch to branch, here, there, everywhere, with incredible and relentless energy—pecking upon the woody parts of the tree, searching for dormant insects, eggs, perhaps, or cocoon cases. Their long winter feathers, fully fluffed out, came down so far that the featherless feet were all covered. Having no snowshoes, they kept to low twigs and branches so as always to have a take-off for flying, for if they alight on soft snow they must fly straight up to get out of it, an exhausting and difficult thing to do. Their small chittering voices seemed as anxious as the rest of them; surely only such a miracle of enterprise could have kept these *tiny* birds alive in Ungava. Even as they watched us, they continued to peck diligently. Only when we could almost touch them would they fly away. Dangers arising from man are probably suspected, but the dangers of wind, cold and hunger are very real to an Ungava chickadee and are always near.

We allowed ourselves to follow the snowshoe tracks of a trapper back to the small knoll in a clearing where stood the telltale stone, looming large and too natural. The large stone is always a trap-marker for a white fox set, and the certain trap indication is a careful tuft of lichen planted at its base; the snow-sunk steel jaws are waiting just below.

"Want to pick that little plant?" Jack asked hopefully. But we were already enlightened. One of the geologists had dug some green moss out and got a trap suddenly fastened into his fingers.

Once used to the air and walking swiftly, we had found the day short and pleasant. Not coldness but our hunger finally turned us home. We had not eaten since breakfast. Already at only two o'clock the yellow sun had taken on an orange cast and only its top showed above the horizon. The earlier shadows were now much longer, darkly streaming behind every hump and thicket. The whole land was alive with the sunset, and we clumped home through new and strangely peopled snows.

On that same night we began language lessons. Jack was going through Ross' books in a bored way. All of us guessed that he was intending not to think about the plane. It should have been back at Great Whale River by now. The radio was violent with static and the storm below us undeniable.

"Lymburner is cautious," one of us said once. "That's why he's good. He's more likely to wait than to risk a forced landing."

"I'd feel safer making a forced landing with Lymburner than Sunday-flying around an airport with anybody else," I added, but I doubt that Jack heard our remarks. He never said anything.

My Moose Factory parka was decidedly uncomfortable. There was something wrong with the fit of the hood.

"This thing lets in all-outdoors," I told Ross, who looked at me a trifle sadly. He stopped Mary Took-a-Look that night as she was setting the table for supper and said

69

something to her briefly, in Husky, as he turned me slowly around for exhibition. Mary Took-a-Look (a large pink-flowered china sugar bowl grasped tensely between her hands) gave an explosive giggle but eyed me with a passionate comprehension and an eager nodding of her dark head.

"It's all right," said Ross. "She can fix it."

She had not examined me or the parka in any way, but had only looked with glittering eyes, unblinking as a deer or a bird. She took the parka apart after supper, sitting close under the kitchen light for the sewing. We all felt that we should be extraordinarily nice that night to soothe her ruffled feelings after the long subjection to the Swedish cook. Perhaps the excessive number of men in the household had frightened her; certainly she began to dance like a daffodil the moment that they were gone. Daily thereafter, like a dictator, she added power after power unto herself. She surveyed the field each morning with vivid smiles and flouncing eager movements. She smiled upon us with shining teeth and with domineering finger pointed all things out, demanding *"Shoon-a-hauk-peet? Shoon-a-hauk-peet?"* ("What is it?") No-one ever had a more interested teacher than we had in her.

She swept, she cooked, she sewed, with the endlessly vital concentration of a chickadee in all these things. She seemed to find enormous self-satisfaction in any form of activity whatever. Generally speaking, we were the poor plants in her garden, to be lured with light, and she shone upon us like a great warm sun.

I never tried on the remade parka until it was done. She did not deliver it directly to me. She handed it to Ross, who handed it back to me. I slipped into it on the spot; it fitted perfectly. The surprise I felt at this deft accomplishment suddenly brought back a word of west-coast Husky. *"Pitchok!"* ("Good!") I cried.

At which the little pee-marie went off into a perfect ditcher of giggles, clasping her hands tightly together over her breast and rocking back and forth swiftly in her

70

hard, straight chair.

"*Ee-e! Ee-e!*" ("Thank you! Thank you!") she cried rapturously.

But Ross was not impressed. "Most of them call it *peeruk,*" he said shortly, "over here."

The eighteenth was a dark, gloomy day with no sun, but what a happy day, for Lymburner returned on a strong south wind, which meant a tail wind and a fast easy trip. Now we had all our food and equipment with us at last, and looking at him, we all wondered why we ever questioned his making it. Jack felt no doubt the happiest of all, but he kept his poker-face and made little to-do.

Lymburner, with characteristic thoughtfulness, had suspected that Great Whale River would be cut off by wind from the last radio broadcast and had carefully recorded all messages sent to us. There was a glow all over me at what Sally said, although it was a very simple message, "All is well at home."

With happy hearts and renewed energy, Doutt and I continued packing for the dog trip, enjoying the merry sound in all the voices, the air of vitality that takes over any place where Lymburner goes. A constant phrase comes to my mind when I think of him, even now, "Weather permitting. . . ." It was a stock phrase of the trade, but whenever he said it it took on vital meanings, symbolizing the perfect sanity with which he apparently governed his life. Magnificently he controlled everything, including himself, seeming to work with, not against, even the forces of violent Nature. The last sound I heard that night before I slept was Lymburner's cheerful voice as he bade good night to the one remaining geologist: "Weather permitting, we shall leave tomorrow."

On 20 January, Lymburner took off right after breakfast into a beautiful clear sky, with bright sun, no wind and the temperature at only zero. Jack was quiet, as usual.

"So long, Jack" I said, shaking hands at the last

71

moment, and feeling strangely sad, as if we had known each other for a long time. The primus burners roaring under the plane were making an old and familiar sound—a sound that used to mean camping out in an Alberta winter—white snow and the odour of forests. Now it means also sunny flashes of metal and the warm oil smells of an Arctic airplane.

It was our last chance for months, perhaps, to send messages Outside. Doutt and I hastily added a few more words to our unfinished letters. Some Eskimos had gathered on the river boisterously surrounding the plane, while their dogs, heartened by the presence of their masters, circled it freely, sniffling it at every point. At the first cough of the engine the dogs skittered in all directions, and when the propeller began to whirl, the Eskimos scattered too. Hands were shaken once again all around. The three men mounted to their places. On gaining altitude, the big plane turned back as before, and went roaring over us, headed south—to Fort George—to Pittsburgh—to "the world." Lymburner waved farewell with the wings, and the silver glinted, dwindled and died in the distance. They were gone.

From his safe retreat a watching Husky dog howled mournfully. We turned to look at the same small group of Eskimos. Laughingly, and perhaps to entertain us, they began to run a few steps, mockingly graceful, and then to flap their arms like wings as if to take off. A train or an automobile would probably scare them half to death, but they have seen a plane several times before—often enough to feel little fear of it. They show a sort of affection for it, in fact. They fondly touch its cold, shining sides as it stands idle, and when it leaves they chase after it wholeheartedly.

The last touch with the Outside had vanished. Somehow more hopefully than ever before, we climbed back up to the post-house. No more diversions. We had our stuff. Our duty was clear. We must push straight ahead now!

First thing of all, we went to find Old Harold. He is

about 70,[6] and they say he has a lifetime of savings in a bank Outside, but the old interpreter still works and lives frugally. The furnishings in his two-room house were much as Flaherty described them many years ago. The jacket-stove with the oven on top still stands in the living-room with the few odd pictures and a couple of chairs. Old Harold, as shy as a fawn and as embarrassed as a native woman at any meeting with strangers (just "bushed," I might have said, if I had known nothing of his history), would not even let his picture be taken. The one I jokingly took caught him blushing and laughing and trying to hide his face.

Old Harold's wife (sister of the famous Eskimo, Old Husky Bill), whom Flaherty recorded in 1914 as wearing "white-man's shoes," now wears Eskimo *komiks*, and whereas with Flaherty she "sat and stared into space," she now flees from visitors and hides in the bedroom, where only her sleeping-bag lies on the floor.[7]

We soon arranged with Old Harold that he should act as interpreter when the time came for us to interview the Eskimo Kooke, and at last, despite his excessive self-consciousness, Old Harold, with sad face and lowered eyes, began reminiscing. Yes, he said, there were many more natives when he first came to the post at Great Whale River. Fifty years ago, when he was a younger man (here he smiled at us delicately), 70 or 80 Eskimo families used to camp on the post plains every summer, and the Indians too came to the coast then in very great numbers. Not just a few, like today! None of the natives then, said the old man, needed clothes from the Company; they all dressed in the skins of caribou. None of them needed tea then or flour or tobacco; they lived on fish and seal and the dried meat of the caribou and the berries that the caribou uncovered on the hills and dug out of the snow with their heavy hoofs. At first, said Old Harold, they wanted to trade fur only for the kettles in the post store. Then they began to want guns and ammunition. As long as the caribou lasted, they wanted nothing more. But now, bit by bit, said the old man, the natives will die, for the animals are going, and even seals are not plentiful. He seemed so moved by the recitation that I was almost sorry we had persuaded him to tell us the familiar story.

On the fifth day of our stay at Great Whale River, Kooke* finally came—a neat, waddling, solemn-faced old Eskimo full of soft doubts and murmured indignations. Mary Took-a-Look always knew when anyone was coming. A visitor could be seen for miles as he crossed that big white plain northwest of the post. Ross took us at once to the porch shed to shake Kooke's hand. We gave the Eskimo a fervant *"chimo"* and unpretended pleasure. Mary Took-a-Look was ready with the inevitable tea. The fat, grey granite pot standing in the centre of the squatting circle of natives made a great show of steam in the cold air of the shed. The Eskimo who had carried Ross' message to Kooke was drinking there, as well.

While he waited for his tea, the elderly Kooke took from his pants pocket a plug of pressed tobacco and shaved it off solemnly into his hand. Rolling it up delicately, he pressed it into his pipe bowl, gingerly, with his index finger. This pipe was as neat and clean as the rest of him, the tin lid (with which all Northern pipes are fitted against the wind) shining brightly. No doubt he had scrubbed himself up for the occasion, for among all the Eskimos that I have ever seen, he remains the only one to be so thoroughly distinguished. The pee-marie stood in the kitchen tensely waiting to see what would happen, a wide grin of expectation on her face.

We went inside and left the men to drink their tea. Ross had sent a man down for Old Harold, who came presently in a peaked-front cap of wool, the kind that we used to call a "Buffalo Bill." He was so tall, and so thin, in a very full parka that seemed much too big for him, with

*This was the same Kooke who had been taken by Mr. Todd from Great Whale River to Port Harrison by dog team in 1933.

his scraggly grey beard, and long, thick, softly curling, silvery hair, that I found him almost as picturesque as Kooke himself. Old Harold pulled his cap off as he entered the kitchen and with excessive show of shyness murmured "Hello."

"Well," said Ross, "let's go and get it over with."

Everyone followed Ross into the "office." Doutt and I were followed by Old Harold, who was followed by the natives. Ross sat in his desk chair, his poor abused shoulders bearing the burden as he sat, and his feet hoisted onto the table. I sat on the table edge and Doutt leaned against it. Old Harold and the natives sat like a row of schoolboys on the long bench, and Kooke's handsome young son showed his worldliness by the adroitness with which he rolled a cigarette. I began to feel a little sick as the conference haltingly progressed. Kooke was much too old to be travelling into the interior in winter and Ross had been quite right about the Eskimos. Kooke murmured in soft, tentative sounds, but the emphatic shaking of his head was a definite negative in any language.

"You see, it's because he won't walk," said Old Harold, shaking his own head sadly.

"No Eskimo will walk," explained Ross decisively. "Not when he can possibly help it!"

"Why did he agree to, then, in the first place?" Doutt demanded to know.

"He didn't understand you," answered Old Harold. "He thought that you would all fly in—clear in—in your own airplane, and then fly out again."

I had a mental vision of the old man's disappointment, the humiliation that he would feel on returning home without this long-boasted adventure. It was no wonder that he felt indignant. A dream of two years' standing was now rudely ended.

Ross was thoughtful for several minutes while the old Eskimo eyed us suspiciously, murmuring from time to time further excuses. His dogs, Old Harold relayed to us, were poor. Very poor! Coast Eskimos, he continued, had never shot seals in the inland. He would not let his young boys, moreover, risk such a hard trip. He himself had made two attempts to penetrate to Seal Lakes in winter and had had to turn back both times. In all his life he had really been there only once. And, besides, he had injured his hand! This last is the most impressive excuse that a Northern native knows. *To have an injured hand* is to be practically useless for everything!

We took out a new gun and let Kooke handle it. His delight was pitiful. It was a seal gun,* which Mr. John B. Semple of Pittsburgh built for us. They all showed a pathetic pleasure at feeling the gun in their hands. Yes, it was a good seal gun; yes, it would kill the seal all right; yes, it would be a very fine thing for a hunter to have. The boys were absorbed in the study of it. It would be just right, they said.

But in the end they gave the gun back to us. If they all died at the Seal Lakes, Kooke told Old Harold soberly, even the new gun would not help. He had made up his mind and that was all there was to it. But he continued for quite a little while, just to talk. He felt that he had not been properly informed in the first place, that he was wasting his time, that his rights had somehow been violated, that whether he went inland with us or not he had a right to complain about it. He would think it over, he said. The final upshot of the interview was that he would go away now, and later he would let us know.

"It's my opinion," said Ross thoughtfully, when the hunters had gone, "that Kooke never meant to go in the first place. I suspect that he grew tired of the discussion and just began nodding his head to get rid of you." Doutt and I were listening dumbfounded. "They'll all do that,

*This seal gun does not follow the pattern of any other harpoon gun. Mr. Semple used an old .30 US Army rifle and constructed a harpoon that fitted like a sleeve over the barrel. Thus, by not injuring the rifling, it made a dual-purpose gun—it could be used to throw a harpoon or to fire a rifle cartridge.

you know. They hate much conversation. They are only interested in the immediate moment, and the quickest way to stop a white man's talking is usually just to smile and nod the head. They know that much," said Ross, and added proudly, "they're *not dumb!*"

The more we thought of it, the more probable Ross' guess began to seem. After all, as Ross said, Eskimos (although they might be dirty and procrastinating and untruthful) were never dumb. We were in a pretty pickle and we knew it.

We should have to throw all our old plans overboard and begin again. Old Harold was of Ross' opinion. The Eskimos were unfit for the interior because their heavy *komatiks* would mire in the loose snow of the woodlands, which would also be impassable for the dogs. The Richmond Gulf Indians who went inland occasionally always travelled very light, pulling their own toboggans, each carrying about 125 pounds. They were said to live largely on the country, hunting ptarmigan and catching fish.

"If you think we'd better try it," Doutt told Ross finally, "I think we ought to travel with the Indians." But even so, Ross was not encouraging.

"There are very few of them," he said. "It's not easy to find one who knows how to take you to the Seal Lakes region. There is a chance, however," Ross added, "that Daniel Petacumeshcum might be here any time. He might know how. You can wait and see."

Pet-a-cu-*mesh'*-cum! The very name was appalling. He would be a strong character with a name like that, I felt sure. If a good man, he would be splendid. If a bad man, then a bad one indeed. At least he was a good hunter, Ross said, and one who knew the country. As to when he might be expected, Ross smiled wearily as he answered—"Can't say. You'll just have to wait."

We waited.

Later in the day, one Indian trapper came. He was unacquainted with the Seal Lakes country except by rumour. That seemed to be all he wanted of it. But he knew that Little Whale River was partly open still. No-one would be travelling inland on that waterway, and, like Ross, he had heard that Seal Lakes hunters always turned inland only at Richmond Gulf.

Three Richmond Gulf Indians were expected in a few days—a few weeks perhaps or a few months, in this country. We could wait, and go on waiting. There was nothing else for it.

We concentrated on getting into condition. I seized the opportunity for studying the birds around the immediate territory and we worked Ross and Mary Took-a-Look almost to death, learning what we could of the east-coast Eskimo language, looking forward to the spring months on the Belchers. Of Indian words, we learned only what seemed necessary for use on the trail and let it go at that.

"George can talk to the Indians," we used to say to him at the bridge table in the evening. "We can't pay him if he doesn't do *something*." And George would laugh his short little laugh and have to begin all over the calculation of his cards. Although self-important like most guides, George was a pretty good fellow. I haven't found many guides who can take any ribbing. George loved to play bridge, and after Jack left, Jeff and Ross and George and I used to make a nightly foursome over the cards, sitting around the bare dining-table under the lamp, the round belly of the hot stove glowing beside us, the wind howling, in emphasis of our snugness. Doutt didn't much like the game, but when we needed him, would obligingly play.

It was strange about Ross. He never struck me as being in the least interested in the personal habits of the natives, but at any mention of a vice or weakness in them, he would show plainly that he had been struck in a tender spot. He had a highly critical and academic mind, and I think that he lumped the natives as a race, all together, feeling for them a great objective admiration, and having a secret loyalty toward everything that meant Ungava. I was slowly coming to understand why.

It seems incredible, as I look back now, that we could have been trapped for a solid month at the post at Great Whale River. It was a feverish month, in which our spirits paralleled the erratic weather. We alternately hoped and despaired. We turned this way and that in a cage of wind and snow. Sometimes we sat in the house watching wild flurries of driving rime, like sleet, which constituted the world that day at Great Whale River, and were darkly hopeless and resigned. But when the wind died, we ploughed once more among the house-high drifts of hills, feeling the growing strength of our bodies and pretending that it was all for the good.

The twenty-first was our hardest single day of waiting. The drifter that had been locking us in had gone in the night. There was bright sun and a cloudless sky. Our hours on that day were all strangely intensified, for two Richmond Gulf Indians, one of them Daniel Petacumeshcum, had come to the post-house at dawn and Ross had made diplomatic arrangements for us all to have an interview in the evening.

That afternoon, I took a restless and solitary walk, crossing from the post-house, on the north bank of the river, over to the south bank. The sun shone brightly in the pale sky above me, a sky so cloudless and thin that it looked like water. Both north and south banks of Great Whale River rise sharply, and as I walked down along the swooping south shore for about a mile and a half, snow sometimes tumbled over to the very river's edge; many times a slope spotted with bushes would show fresh ptarmigan tracks. The south bank was thick with willows, the willow twig being apparently the chief and perhaps only food of the Great Whale River ptarmigan throughout nine months of the year. Once two lonely white birds huddled together on the very edge of a high bank like a perfect picture for a grocery-store calendar, and were silhouetted against the yellowing sun. The winding tracks of a hunting fox threaded the thickets, following closely the feeding grounds of the ptarmigan as fox tracks always do in bush country, and several times I found blood and bits of ptarmigan feathers and scattered ptarmigan entrails. Far beyond, out in the Bay waters, the great pressure ridges bulged up in tremendous, strange shapes, startling to the fancy, the only thing that broke the monotony of the wide flowing whiteness of Great Whale River. The river was now all frozen over except for a few rapids at the very mouth, but as late this year as Christmas Day, somebody told me, Eskimos had paddled in on it to celebrate at the post. By keeping to the ice I was able to walk without snowshoes, and my whole body felt grateful and light with the unaccustomed freedom. I scarcely knew that I had any feet. They were in soft skin boots, well mattressed with the inside duffle-moccasins and several pairs of wool socks. They were "snuggled," I thought cheerfully, not "shod." That same old eerie feeling that I have often had when alone in free places again came over me—and was not unpleasant. Once a group of twenty ptarmigan sat in a motionless union, as if all were carved in full relief out of a single piece of marble.

My mind was mostly on the coming conference with Daniel and his companion from Richmond Gulf. I tried to imagine how it would seem now to be already back from the Seal Lakes region and prepared to cross the ice bridge to the Belcher Islands!

"Cold?" Doutt asked me anxiously as I came in.

"Cold!" I answered with contempt, "of course not. I'm too *hot*!"

"Me too," said Doutt. Then we looked at each other. It was all right to be hot after two or three hours, coming home to the cozy house at Great Whale River, but it would never do to be hot on the interior trail.

"We better get busy on the clothes again," Doutt decided rather sadly. "There are a lot of things wrong with mine, come to think of it."

That night, the sky was shot in all directions by the

Northern lights. They formed a huge vivid arch across the heavens, an arch that remained arched but danced and wavered incessantly in feverish movements. And what sounds they made! Like hot, crackling fires or the heavy lashing of whips. They were just beginning to open up on us when the two Richmond Gulf Indians arrived, waiting ceremoniously in the shed with Old Harold, who had come along with them as interpreter. Almost at once the interview began.

Did they know the way to the Seal Lakes region?

Perhaps so. Perhaps not—although they had both been there, in summer.

But they had not been there in winter?

Perhaps so, perhaps not.

Would they be interested in guiding our expedition?

While they sat in deliberation, our conference was interrupted by the entrance of another Indian, an Eastern Cree from the post settlement across the river. He eyed Doutt and me briefly without apparent reaction and then began a low musical harangue with the two Richmond Gulf Indians, in which only the word *undowksin* (sick) was intelligible to me. That the conference was at an end, however, seemed certain, for our two conferees were pulling up the hoods of their parkas and all the Indians were at the door before Old Harold had time to explain to us. Old Harold rumbled out at them with his thunderous steady rolling of words, but they answered only *Wabneetchy*. Old Harold sighed, eyeing us sympathetically, but shyly.

"They say you must wait. They will come back tomorrow." (We must always wait!)

We shook hands all around, and then with no motions wasted the Indians were gone. An old Cree with a gangrenous leg, who had been much talked of since we came to the post, was about to die. His dying wish was to see these Richmond Gulf Indians.

"It will not be long now," said Old Harold, with an aged man's natural sadness and translating the Indian's

81

word for death very literally, "before he will be going off to the land where something never lives." His face was dim and faded, like a fine old etching. Then he grew shy again, as if he had said too much.

Ross said the gangrene case was typical. The sick Indian developed a leg infection. Ross treated it, but the cure moved slowly. One day the Indian's relatives secretly decided that they could drive out the disease with the ancient and mystical ceremony of burning. They packed the leg with red-hot stones and baked the flesh, literally, to drive the poison away. Gangrene had set in immediately and swiftly spread up through the thigh, so that even the relatives now admitted that the Indian was done for. There was already much mourning and visiting. He would surely die! The man's family would then be furnished with a burial box made of lumber and a sheet in which to wrap the body. A burial service would be read, in an attempt to approximate the ministrations of the Church, and the sealed box would lie in state in the snows until the ground thawed in spring when it could be buried.

"They will come again tomorrow," said Old Harold and would not stay with us any longer. His old wife, an Eskimo ancient to whom he had never tried to teach his language, was at home alone. He was embarrassed and decrepit, a strange, effeminized old man, "a devout Christian" according to the bishop, and indispensable to the bishop's yearly Indian service. He was a man of a hundred stories, I felt sure. The Northern lights had now faded and were not very interesting. We watched the sky hopefully for a little while, then, chilled and grumbling, went to bed.

These Indians are breathtakingly abrupt, forthright and of few words. What a contrast to our discussions with Kooke the Eskimo! The next morning, without any preamble, Daniel Petacumeschcum came in with Old Harold to say, yes, that he would go, but he flatly laid down the conditions, permitting no further discussion: we would provide food for his family while he was away; we would furnish him with two Indian helpers; we would hire some Indians *especially* acquainted with the region to act as guides. He did not ask or suggest or consider. He *told* us. It was his ultimatum. He would leave immediately for his own home on Richmond Gulf, where we would join him later, accompanying an "expert guide" whom Daniel declared was about to arrive now at Great Whale River—just any moment!

Since Richmond Gulf was the nearest Hudson's Bay Company outpost to the north and was our first objective, this plan seemed sensible, for Daniel, going ahead, could himself collect the necessary Indian helpers. Daniel seemed certain that a good Indian guide was on his way right now to Great Whale River. If we could all get up to Richmond Gulf, we could all proceed inland at once. Even Ross could find no flaw in the arrangement. Our main load of provisions could start now and go up to Richmond Gulf on the frozen Bay safely and swiftly by dog sled. There was a post Eskimo here at Great Whale River whom Ross would engage to take the first sled load for us. The more we considered it, the better it seemed.

Ross strongly advised us to accept Daniel's offer. That Daniel was competent there seemed no doubt. His manner was "dispatch" itself. Having laid down the law in less than five minutes, Daniel rose and desired to go.

"There have been words enough," he explained to Ross bluntly. "Soon the day will have been spent in talking."

At George's swift translation of Daniel's words we secretly agreed. Things could not move too fast now to suit us, not that I myself felt complacent about the prospect of going anywhere with Daniel. His abruptness was grotesque, as if there were something unbalanced in him. We relied nevertheless on Ross' assurance and I myself was getting into a reckless mood. Daniel's conditions were not unreasonable. It was only that he had not asked us in the usual bargaining way what we had to offer, but had stated flatly and proudly, *Indwyten!* (I must have!)

We came to a hasty agreement, afraid in fact that if we didn't, Daniel might decide he had already been bothered with us sufficiently. Ross was pleased. I was pleased. Old Harold was grateful to have been of assistance. Doutt began forming new schemes for the packing.

"The Indians call the Upper Lake"—actually seeming *lower* on our maps, because it lies farthest south — *Manasquo-a-chic-sakgaheegan,* Old Harold explained, in a rare moment of fulsomeness, and helped me to spell it out. "It means 'Seal Lake *in the Woods*'; Lower Lake, which lies up in the barren land, they call *Achic-o-sakgaheegan*—just plain 'Seal Lake.' "

For the next twenty days, Doutt and I were scarcely aware of anything local. Our minds were all out with the loads of food that went up in relays of sleds to Richmond Gulf, and on Daniel Petacumeshcum, the Richmond Gulf Indian who was supposed to be now collecting helpers at the Richmond Gulf settlement. The "expert guide" whom Indian Daniel had spoken of never came, but that didn't surprise us. One learns that at Great Whale River there are few surprises. We decided to accompany the last food-load and the two sled-drivers, who would probably be Eskimos.

But things locally important did continue to happen. The old Indian with the gangrenous leg soon died and the body rested in the mission church while a coffin was made. Mary Took-a-Look, usually so cheerful, had a crying fit one night. She ran out into the driving wind without any wraps on and stayed there for two hours, weeping. The old men among the Eskimos insisted that she only needed a husband to beat her "more than a little." I felt sorry for her, thinking that post life had unfitted her for her own people, but she was laughing again gaily after a few hours. Sometimes I listened to

George and Ross in conversation, about Indians' methods of dentistry, for instance: they mix black gunpowder with a little pain killer that Ross keeps at the post, then roll the mixture inside a bit of cotton and stick the wad into the aching cavity. The Indians mix black powder with dog meat to cure the dogs of worms, and make a soothing poultice of gunpowder and water for chapped skin.

I sealed up my notes in letter-size packages from time to time, and hopefully addressed them to Sally. Although mail comes to the Great Whale River post officially twice a year—by dog team in March and in August on the supply boat—there is always the possibility that some plane may fly through or that someone will make a forced trip by sled down to Fort George, and someone from Fort George make a trip to Rupert's House,[8] and the mail get carried eventually to Moose Factory and the railroad at Moosonee. It is *noblesse oblige* that anyone travelling on the east Bay coast shall be a willing packhorse for everybody's letters.

25th January
Just watched a drifter coming—like a silver cyclone. The sky darkens with clouds, the snow sweeps up in sheets on the driving wind. The tops of the bared rocks become crowned with swirls as though whitely smoking. A haze covers us all and the whirling mass moves out across the plain too thick to see through, and about breast high.

26th January
Saw grasses where red-polls had fed, but could find no birds there. Native boys reported seeing what was probably a gyrfalcon, chasing a ptarmigan. They called it a grouse hawk. Cook killed a snowy owl near the post recently.

27th January
A puppy had yelped at night ever since we came. When

we used to open the door for him, he would back off and curl up in the snow again, in true Husky dog fashion, but after last night's storm he has sneaked inside today all worn out, and now is stretched on the floor at my feet. He was born much too late, they say, just after the first snowfall.

31st January
Nothing but storms, with false respites between. The poor birds are in hiding most of the time. When they come out, they are famished. Even the gun means nothing to most of them. They just peck away insistently. . . . I saw wolf tracks yesterday, and heard a mournful howl.

2nd February
Storm or no storm, Sam Crow left yesterday with another load of our food. From here to Richmond Gulf outpost for only $25.00 in Hudson's Bay Company credit! . . . Reindeer lichens and cranberry plants have been exposed by the wind in quite a few places, frozen solid, but still in bright red and green colours, just as they were when the first frost caught them. Sun so bright that even the lemmings are out on the surface, their burrows clearly in evidence. Red squirrel tracks showed up today, here and there.

(Our Husky puppy has lice, which are inactive out of doors, but inside the house, near the stove, they come to life and nearly drive him crazy.)

13th February
For two weeks, only wind and snow! We are marooned again! I have been hunting birds anyway. We walk all we can, to keep our muscles flexible and test our clothes. We hear wild tales of the great speed of the Indians, and I have visions of Daniel Petacumeshcum watching me stolidly while I sink into a snowdrift, and then proceeding to Seal Lakes, as agreed upon, but

without me. I found a raven, scarcely expected since caribou no longer come here, and there can't be many carcasses to eat. We have news of an unmapped river, which the Indians know about and travel on, inland. It has its source, they say, in one of the Seal Lakes. It is only rumour, but that is all anything is here. We are more and more hopeful. One Indian says that *kasagea* does not taste quite like the salt-water *netchek*.[9] It really sounds like something to go after!

Later

The front vestibule is filled with a snowbank, a good drift that has seeped in all around the never-used door. It storms from the south tonight and the wind is strong but not cold. The old gangrenous Indian who died was a famous maker of seal nets, and his daughter Maggie is now making us two of them. In making the net, Maggie uses no fishnet needle, as we expected, but holds the net strands on a flat piece of wood, and keeps the thread in her hand. She only ties the knots with an ordinary needle—the simplest imaginable method.

Later

We may be leaving soon for Richmond Gulf. We hug the fire at night, and listen to the radio. With no drifter and no aurora borealis, we sometimes hear something. Reception is usually awful, but still a radio here is so important that the men will go to almost any length to have it. The enormous aerial over the post-house keeps Ross fixing it. Talk of war with Japan or Germany seems ludicrous, like an impossible dream. We seem to sit on a high seat watching life go by. *Kasagea* is the only thing that's important. I begin to like Ross a lot, and to appreciate his detachment.

The wind-blown snow stays comfortably hard, but under the trees, even on snowshoes, I sink down at least six or seven inches. Hard going! But we're getting used to it!

87

15th February

Yesterday it was bright—42 below zero. Some excitement at breakfast because Mary Took-a-Look found hypo-solution in her pitcher after Doutt's film developing, and thinking it water poured the stuff into the pancakes. They were like rubber. We are crazy with impatience. I am trying Christian Science. How can we possibly make it in and out again in time for the Belchers! Another wind tonight, and the snow driving along over everything! We plan to leave day after tomorrow!

17 February 11 o'clock in the morn.

My last note before I leave this package with Ross. Three teams of Richmond Gulf Eskimos arrived yesterday, and one returns to Richmond Gulf this morning. George is already there (at the Company outpost), and the Indian boy, Ross' helper named Boyshish, is with him. Ross has reminded us several times lately that 21 Indians, caught at Seal Lakes in a hard drifter, died there of starvation in 1930. (Only three survived from the crowd. The child Boyshish was one of them.) But we are sure that we'll come out of it with our skins all right—and *kasagea's* too.

COASTAL JOURNEY TO RICHMOND GULF: OF THE KOMATIK AND THE TUPEK

It was still dark at six o'clock. Doutt and I lit candles to dress by, taking up our bed-rolls and packing everything ready for strapping onto the *komatik*. We left the room just as we had found it. Downstairs the pale yellow kitchen light by which Mary Took-a-Look had cooked our breakfast made but a faint impression against the greyish light of just-before-morning beyond the windows. At that hour the living-room was a bleak sight. We bolted our breakfast, saying almost nothing, but thinking hard.

There could be no turning back for anything forgotten. Every moment we expected to hear the soft voices of Ekumiak and Mikiuk and the "scrapping" of dogs, but we finished breakfast and lingered impatiently over a second cup of tea without sight of them. It was eight o'clock before they came.

Ross unlocked the warehouse, and at the first sound of voices, a Husky dog of seemingly great proportions with his bushy fur, bolted straight out through a square twelve-inch window. I measured the thing to make sure! How he squeezed through it we couldn't explain, but there he came as we watched.

Inside, the smell of seal meat was heavy in the air. The thieving Husky had been having an orgy, perhaps all night. The barrel of meat chunks that Ross always kept in one corner of the warehouse for his own dogs was almost empty, and since Ross' dogs were already overdue from the hard run to Moose Factory, he was worried about it. He had allowed the driver six weeks for the journey—which should have been long enough. When the team did come, the dogs would be hungry; now there must be more hunting for seal meat. Mikiuk looked pleased that his dog had meat in its stomach. Ekumiak looked guilty, as if he himself had eaten it.

Eventually we began packing the big eighteen-foot *komatik*. When Mikiuk and Ekumiak began to bring on their provisions, our first light load of 550 pounds increased in an hour to about 1200. Mikiuk had but six dogs. The thing had to stop! The Eskimos were more excited about it than we were. Were they to have to walk? The men clucked about among the things like two flurried chickens, but finally decided that everything must be taken. Day mounted in the sky. The sun painted us in pinks for a few lurid moments and then burst out in a golden flood.

Eight hundred to a thousand pounds of freight is commonly pulled by eight dogs, but a load of 1200 pounds is extremely heavy. Even strong, well-trained dogs, eight to the pack, are not put to this task very often, although of course it is the condition of the road as well as the weight that dictates how much stuff a *komatik* should carry.

Nowadays sled runners are usually wooden planks prepared by the Hudson's Bay Company and sold at the posts. In the old days sled runners were made by the natives from driftwood and even of bone, but now modern runners have displaced the oldtime ones.

The Company runners come shod with steel, but by far the greatest speed and smoothness for a *komatik* is still attained by preparing plank runners in the Eskimo way. It is called *earthing*. This is done by moistening peat—decayed leaf-mould from the muskegs—and smearing it along the runner, where it freezes solidly and can be smoothed to form a fine, icy surface. A sudden hit will destroy the edge of the peat or break it off in chunks, but on smooth snow earthed runners are invaluable. Almost no friction meets the sled on peat-shod runners, and great speed can be made and heavy loads easily pulled by very few dogs. Earthing is still the common practice in Ungava. It is always resorted to by careful and skilful Eskimos under the right conditions.

Urine—which, like most products in the Arctic, is seldom wasted—is the common solvent used on the trail for the earthing process. It is admirable for moistening the peat—since, when used fresh, it is of exactly the right temperature, and does not need to be heated at all. Successive layers of wet peat are frozen onto the runners, until a ballooning bulge, looking somewhat like a lumpy rubber tire, results. When planed with a knife, the sides of the bulge achieve a nice curve and the bottom a fine smoothness. Lastly, the runner is "iced". A hare's foot or a piece of hairy dog fur is dipped into the warm liquid and run swiftly down the length of the runner. When several layers of ice have been added, the earthing is over. The *komatik* has been "shod".

On earthed runners and over smooth surfaces our load

would have bothered nobody, but 1200 pounds over the rocky Bay ice was another story. Our runners were earthed, but no-one expected the earthing to last long. What a fussing and a funning those two volatile Eskimos made! — but I am sure they enjoyed it. How important they made everything seem! Gradually we white people relaxed, as always, and with a sigh of helpless resignation ceased to fret at the steady passage of time.

While the natives tightened up the final lashing—the long sealskin passing over the canvas that protects the load—I paid a final visit to the house and added one more note before I sealed up Sally's letter. I was aware of the warmth and comfort of the room and of one more farewell.

It was 11:05 when we started off. The sky had become overcast. The short journey over the snowy plain before we reached the Bay would be something of a struggle. A strong east wind had risen and there was beginning to be a light fall of snow. We shook hands with Ross, and I felt a touch of shame that it had taken me so long to understand him and a sudden flood of admiration for the quiet resignation with which he accepted Ungava — accepted it sportingly like a gentleman, apparently with no feeling of defeat. It must be pretty hard to "get" Ungava without letting it get you first. Jeff[10] slapped me on the shoulder, partly, no doubt, to keep warm.

"Come again, fellows," he cried heartily.

"So long," I said to Ross, and wished that I dared say more. "Thanks for everything."

"Goodbye," answered Ross. "Good luck to you."

Ross and Jeff shook hands with Mikiuk too and with Ekumiak, and then Mikiuk began to straighten out the lines and murmur to the beasts as he stepped among them, bending to them swiftly here and there. The dogs yipped and panted, some sitting in the snow facing us with tongues hanging, some standing up with tails high and waving excitedly. At last all was ready!

"*Wheet, wh-eet!*" cried Mikiuk, which is the Eskimo

91

equivalent of "mush" or "get along". The boss dog in the middle gathered his muscles, haunches low, front legs spraddled, and dug his toes in hard for the pull. All hands gave a push to overcome the first friction, and immediately the sled lunged forward. We were off. We waved again. It was very warm—ten degrees above zero.

Walking behind, I saw that the shed was leaving two brown tracks in the snow. In the sudden warmth of the weather, the icing on the sled runners was already going bad. We all looked back again and waved to Ross, who stood watching. We could see Roy Jeffries halfway to the house. "Be a good idea," I could imagine his saying, as he slapped his mittened hands together, "to get a cup of coffee."

Perhaps with cold and waiting, anyone would get a little fuzzy. *Kasagea* always seemed much more mythical in Ungava than it had seemed in Pittsburgh. Just to keep on following somebody, and to forget the black blisters popping out on the skin from the cold, and to take pleasure in the thousand strange sights to be seen if only the eyes didn't burn so—that much seemed really clear. Oh yes—Richmond Gulf! At Richmond Gulf would at last begin the turning inland—the Great Adventure! Strange that after so many weeks in Ungava the turning inland was still on some day beyond this one, still off in that ever-vague time that is a Northern tomorrow.

Richmond Gulf was a week away everybody predicted, and rightly. The orange-brown track of the earth-packed runners on our *komatik* streaked the white landscape behind us with a wavering path, while we trudged along watching the sled's loose-jointed motion and hearing the slight "woofing" sound it made. It seemed to be the only sound in the world and the only motion.

"*Ra!*" cried Mikiuk once, "*ra, ra,*" as he coaxed the dogs around a hump. The snowfall was increasing, the sky grey, the sun bleary, but the wind, we felt gratefully, was dying down. We gradually descended to Bay level, losing sight of the white frame buildings with their bright red trimming, of the two high posts and the twanging aerial wires between them spanning and paralleling the roof, of the motionless figure of Ross and the climbing figure of Jeff, of everything, in fact, that meant Great Whale River. For a long time after, only our party and the snowflakes moved upon that vast and mournful horizon.

With *ra* (to the right) and *ouk* (to the left), we followed each other forward throughout the rest of the morning —white fields, white sky in every direction. We travelled northeast about 50 or 60 degrees magnetic east, averaging two and a half miles an hour, and as soon as we could, entered the protection of the long, lake-like, sparsely wooded Manitounuk Sound.

In the Sound, where it should have been easier, it so happened that it wasn't. The snow grew more and more heavy throughout the day and the dogs drove us crazy. *Us,* I say, not Mikiuk and Ekumiak. They were not in the least bothered. I can see it all yet: *Now* what has happened? What is the matter? Why don't these east-coast cake-eaters ever carry a whip? (For the dogs are flashing their heads around following the system of the leader, all stopping dead in the snow and sitting down on their haunches! Can't a man ride for two minutes when he's absolutely exhausted? The Eskimos shake their heads sadly. It seems that a man can't!)

Those dogs are uncanny. When a load is light, the natives are always riding, but when a load is heavy, the dogs sense the addition of an ounce. They will pull at a dead-weight until there's no strength left in them, but they will not include in their burden anything with its own legs to it. Even when our *komatik* struck a tiny snowbank, the dogs would be flashing their heads around angrily as if to cry, "*Now* what leech is trying to get away with something!"

Drifts deepened by the hour, leaving the overloaded *komatik* often fast in a rut, while we did as much pushing as the dogs did pulling, wrenching and jerking and straining our shoulder muscles, "working" the sinking and snow-sotted runners. (We had made no bargain for such labour, but we preferred it to wintering in Manitounuk Sound!)

When a *komatik* is stuck there is but one way to dislodge it. After a good side-to-side shoving of the sled, the driver gathers up the main dog-trace so that all dogs feel lines that are taut. Then the driver gives the signal — a sudden up-jerk of the trace — and then at once he lets go of it. The dogs know what is needed and lunge forward with a rush. Every man too shoves, all in unison, and off goes the sled once more into motion (or let us hope!). More times than I like to remember, the dogs sat there on their tails calmly panting and looking back at our patient efforts as we shoved on the load from side to side, with an un-doglike cynical expression like a wry human smile. At such times I took personal pleasure in seeing the driver at last take the trace up and make them, tired or not, help to jerk the thing free.

Near evening there was little speed in them. Sometimes—to incite them to chase him—Mikiuk would run on ahead, but the dogs were half-hearted, seeming to recognize that it was only Mikiuk. As a last resort—and saved for emergencies since it worked without failing—Mikiuk would throw his mitt down and kick it along the snow. Apparently, even if he dies from exertion a Husky dog *must* go after such a thing! But even after a mitt our dogs moved like snails by sundown, howling and crying and making a pitiful fuss.

We lunched at two o'clock on a barren land-point among wind-beaten spruce trees. To leeward of the spruces we built a little fire out of spruce brush and sticks. In a deep snowbank, Ekumiak brushed back the *apputi* (the top six-inch layer of light snow) and found the icy *poka* that could be melted into goodly quantities of water. Bread and jam and tea made our lunch. We felt cheerful, rugged and tremendously refreshed, but the lunchtime went on and on, for Mikiuk, distrusting the

94

wearing runners, *removed the whole load* in order to re-ice them. The whole load! My spirits sank.

There was great palaver between the two Eskimos, with the tea-pail being the obvious centre of discussion. Finally, doubtless out of respect for the white men's notions, Mikiuk grumblingly scooped up more *poka*, stirred up a new fire, and melted more water—instead, I judged, of catching urine in the tea-pail, the only thing we carried that could hold it.

The new icing made going much easier. Surfaces within the Sound varied greatly, and were sometimes so smooth that we were permitted even to steal a tiny ride now and then if we could fool the flagging but still suspicious dogs. We headed from noon on toward a small inland bay with an ancient campsite on its shores. It was 5.45 by the clock when we reached it — already evening. We had finished the first day in the Sound.

Our night camp with the Eskimos was simplified by the fact that four of us occupied one tent. It is a policy generally frowned upon by white men who live among natives, but we felt that our position as strangers in Ungava gave us some leeway to be convenient. Our camp was protected by sharp hills, was in the midst of brush and close to water. A dozen spruce trees were chopped down, the trunks to be used for the shears and ridgepole of our tent and for wood in our stove and the stripped green branches to carpet our floor. While Mikiuk laid in the store of firewood, Ekumiak set up the stove inside and then built a bonfire just beyond the door for cooking the dogs' daily rations of oatmeal and seal grease. Not until his own stomach was full did Mikiuk at last feed the dogs, amid clubbings actually gentle, but with such cries from the dogs that one would think them half-killed. In a few seconds only, the dogs' meal was over. A wolf and a gulp, and a whack or two for the greedy! That was all there was to it. Then, one by one, Mikiuk caught them and tied them to trees for the night, while Ekumiak at the tin stove was cooking two bannocks for tomorrow, frying the thick bread in a skillet with domestic pride. (Bannock, beloved of all Northern natives, is made of flour, grease shortening, baking powder, water and salt.)

That night, fed and weary, we rested on our bed-rolls, while the fresh odour of our spruce-bough flooring permeated everything. Not even the rank seal smell of Mikiuk and Ekumiak disturbed my happy serenity. When the first gallon of tea was gone, we set another to brewing. Once I heard the faint barking of a white Arctic fox, first sign of any wildlife since we left Great Whale River. We tried our new-learned Husky on these two smart and healthy Eskimos whenever there was occasion and with some success—because they were sharp, not because we were clever.

When quite mellow with tea, I tried to tell a whole story, the tale of an adventure that I had once had upon the west coast. Tired and hungry one night, I had found the tilt of a trapper, with the old man inside it cooking his supper. What a smell came to me in the doorway! What a meal I ate that night at the old man's invitation! He was the best cook, bar none, that I have ever met. His bannock especially, I explained to Ekumiak (who nodded and blinked in sober understanding), was second to none.

The tilt had two bunks and at the old man's insistence I had spent the night there, sleeping in the upper bed.

The next morning, after a wonderful sleep and once more expectantly famished, I heard the first morning sounds of a hot, crackling fire. Leaning out of my bunk, I saw the old man crouching to reach under his own. He pulled out the frying pan. I saw something in it. Suddenly I realized that the old trapper had used the skillet as a chamber-pot during the night. With a casual swagger he marched off to the doorway, tossed the waste outside, and returned to his cookstove. There he swabbed out the skillet with a piece of paper and set it on the stove again, cheerfully, to dry.

As I hastily dressed, he was mixing up the batter, and was happily flipping pancakes when I began to make excuses. I had overslept I cried in a fake excitement. There was no time to be lost in breakfast. I must get back *at once* to my own camp!

It was all very jolly. In telling the story I had completely forgotten about Mikiuk and our tea-pail. It never occurred to me at the time that the Eskimos might not be able to see anything strange in the trapper's free habits. But they laughed and laughed. Perhaps the laughing was only at my pantomime—of which there was a great deal. Any Eskimo is a wonderful audience. Who can say what Mikiuk and Ekumiak got from the story?

Our second morning was pitiful. Mikiuk and Ekumiak had but one blanket apiece and were up by 2.30, because they were cold. We couldn't travel in the dark, of course, and so Doutt and I stayed put until daybreak while the two Huskies made their breakfast, moving about with that cheerful stealthiness that is almost worse than death! But we did live through it.

At 6.30 a ptarmigan cry came from back of our camp. It was a fine hour for bird observations, for all birds come out at dawn and are terribly hungry. By the time I was dressed, the eastern sky was changing from a rosy hue to a thin yellow. Thirty yards from our tent door, a flock of 25 ptarmigan fed busily on the tips of widely scattered willow twigs that were scarcely protruding from deep snows. They eyed me cautiously, but went on feeding until the reckless old rooster at last grew wary and with repeated sudden loud squawks gave the general alarm. His cry flushed the whole flock, and off they streaked in a living storm of quivering silver. The sun, lying between two pink-and-yellow sun-dogs, rose from the redness while I finished eating and while our Eskimos re-iced the runner and loaded the *komatik*.

Our second day was a ceaseless round of stops and goes, for the dogs were nervous and highly irresponsible, occasionally wandering off to the side after some scent, and sometimes stopping together just to roll in the snow!

Mikiuk was angry and puzzled and Ekumiak apologetic, but I suspect that the sensitive animals, unused to crowds and to strangers, were keyed up. Perhaps the Eskimos themselves were excited and communicated their own tension to the animals. Still the morning wore on.

We still travelled 60 degrees north, finding within the Sound more and more protection. On either side rocky hills reached an altitude of five hundred to a thousand feet, the knolls were dotted with low groves of spruces and the cuts or valleys often showed spruces as much as 40 feet high. Several species of willows were evident, though half-buried, and on the wind-bared hilltops it was clear that alders and reindeer-lichen made the ground-cover of both slopes and forests. A northern form of andropogan grew on most of the islands, the Sound as a whole being distinctly inland in character in sharp contrast with the raw, boulderish opens of the main Hudson Bay shore. The islands of the Sound, it is true, are high, jagged and rocky, but large stands of trees nestle in the shelters and wind-twisted stragglers are common throughout.

After eleven in the morning, we encountered a southwest wind, and travelled through a snowfall for the rest of the day. We lunched at Paint Islands, unloaded the *komatik* and re-iced the runners. While we waited, another sled, lightly loaded and with nine dogs, flew by us with only a proud lift of the hand in greeting. Mikiuk and Ekumiak stood stock-still, looking after it as far as they could see it go, and then murmured to each other in obvious envy. What a cry rose later from Mikiuk, when just before evening we came once more in sight of those handsome speeders. They were not more than three miles ahead when we camped at sunset.

We made our second camp inland, some distance from the water. Our two Huskies without hesitation dumped off all our supplies onto the unprotected Bay before we proceeded inland with the camping stuff. In vain we objected. The supplies might be stolen while we were sleeping two miles away. But the Eskimos were amused and somewhat noisy in argument. Why shouldn't the heavy things be abandoned? Supplies in the North could *always* be abandoned. No-one *ever* tried to haul a loaded *komatik* through the inland snows.

Our second camp was some four miles from the winter camp of the old Eskimo Kooke whom we had first asked to be our inland guide. No doubt he was still brooding, we thought, about our lack of an airplane. But his son certainly held no grudges, for he put his fur-circled black face, like an apparition, silently between our untied tent-flaps just after supper. Startled, we motioned him in.

"Kach punn" ("I am hungry"), he murmured, smiling expectantly and showing his handsome teeth. Ekumiak smiled at us in turn, spreading his hands wide in a re-signed and expressive gesture. And so, wearily watching and half asleep, we fed Kooke's worldly young offspring on jam and much tea. Our twenty-mile hike through rough ice and wet snow unfitted us to enjoy his company, but we were rid of him shortly, for all he wanted was food. We all had a last congenial cup together, which for us *meant* a cup, and for each of the Eskimos a quart pailful, or, as they said, *"tititallu,"* which means "up to the brim." Ungava *tupeks* on the Hudson Bay coast between Great Whale River Post and Richmond Gulf are so much alike that I will describe but one of them. On the third day we arrived at Boat Opening, and there, flying lonesomely overhead, a raven patiently circled the dark, swift water. The bird seemed very large and very black, and his wings were stiff and slow. He is a defiant bird, refusing even in longest snows to change by one iota the hue of his feathers.

We detoured Boat Opening, unloaded the *komatik* to ice our runners, and were making fine speed indeed when, near sunset, we came to the vicinity of Andrew's *tupeks.* Opposite the north end of Paint Islands we were all laughing for once, because the lead dog had bolted off to a seal hole, followed pellmell by all the others, and the drivers had been completely taken by surprise. But Mikiuk and Ekumiak were rather proud of this wild action, explaining that these dogs hunted with the women, who go out in winter to locate and mark seal holes for their husbands.

There was no evidence that I could see of the existence of a camp. Scatterings of bush and high rising snow-hills seemed the only protection in the locality, and I was entirely surprised when a strange Husky dog rushed out, barking, from under some stragglers. When our dogs growled, the strange dog retreated, and on top of a snow-hill near a scraggly grove the figure of a child appeared. The child had scarcely seen us before it threw up its hands like an old-time actress and disappeared also, while Mikiuk and Ekumiak looked at each other with wide grins of excited satisfaction. Ekumiak turned to us and in a high, silly falsetto mimicked the way any child might cry out the word "strangers!"

A row of Eskimos had begun to gather in ragged dark silhouette against the grey horizon on the top of the snow-hill. All were in blackish clothes, and stood watching us, as inquiring and noncommittal as a pack of buzzards. We neared swiftly. There were about ten women, four men, several children at the women's skirts and, apart from the rest, one crippled boy, holding up one leg and leaning on a crutch. The women's clothes were all drab, dark and ugly. They wore knitted coat-sweaters from the post and thick woollen skirts, which spoke of traffic with the world, but not of prosperity. All stood bareheaded, despite the cold. Their hair was black, stringy, oily and hung haggled, for like the hair of most modern Eskimos it had been cut near the shoulders.

As we all drew together, we frankly studied each other, the women shyly huddled in a group, the men gazing avidly and quite unafraid. The crippled boy had a sharp glance of remarkable intelligence, so remarkable, indeed, on this rag-hung adolescent that it was a little difficult for me to look at anyone else. He was very thin, with a very

100

light-coloured face, a fact that disturbed me at first until I remembered that Eskimos are dark chiefly because they live in the wind. The boy would, of course, stay indoors, being incompetent and fit only for women's work. His critical eye examined us in the most sophisticated way.

With half-smiles of self-consciousness and not a word of greeting, Mikiuk and Ekumiak trudged along officiously, as if pleased with the sensation of the surprise they were springing. We wound on around the hilltop, losing sight of the people, and eventually settled our *komatik* in the near vicinity of the native *tupeks*. As soon as the dogs were unharnessed, our drivers led the way immediately to the native scene. It surprised us to realize that Mikiuk and Ekumiak, for all their fine airs, were already well known in camp. Outside the *tupeks* all the natives were waiting, the men advancing to meet us while the women held back. Everyone present had a *chimo* said to him and every hand was well shaken. The women, shrinking from shyness as we approached them, must have been shrinking from the cold as well.

Most Ungava Eskimo women nowadays do not have parkas of any kind, for their only outdoor work in winter may be the marking of the seals' holes with the sniffing dogs, or some fishing at a chopped-out water hole, or, in the tree country, a little wood-chopping. For these duties they wear the long, black wool man's coat furnished by the Government or endure brief periods of half-freezing in a flimsy post sweater. Since the skirt has displaced the old pants costume for women, they are compelled to spend most of their lives inside the *tupeks* unless they want to freeze.

Greetings over, we went back to build our camp as usual, but we found our dogs snarling and cowering before the vicious "home dogs" who had begun to steal upon them slowly from all sides. Our drivers had to tie the team up and wait among them to prevent fighting until the camp dogs had worn off their first excitement. Indignant glances passed between Ekumiak and Mikiuk, and I had a feeling that the men of Andrew's permitted a closer advance of their brutes than were necessary. But at last, with swinging clubs, the local hunters sent their dogs yelping and skulking to the far side of the *tupeks* among their own trees.

The grounds of Andrew's camp were more than waist-deep in snow, but well-trod paths connected the four *tupeks* and wood-trails had been furrowed out by dragging branches and the trampling with snowshoes. A wide path led up to the hilltop lookout from which the natives had first caught sight of us. Most of the hunters of Andrew's camp were absent on a general seal hunt, but the men available helped brush the floor of our tent. The crippled boy, who stood apart with the women, but close beside the trail that the busy men were using, saw a branch fall near him. The cripple stooped and painfully managed to pick the bough up. Looking at us with a sudden smile on his face, he hobbled a few steps nearer and suddenly tossed it with true aim over onto our floor. It was a touching gesture, in a language that we all knew.

Even our little tent seemed almost as significant as the mushroom of canvas that appears to a stranger to make up the native Eskimo *tupek*. But the Ungava *tupek* is somewhat deceptive. The snow, deeply drifted after November, usually hides the log foundations completely, leaving in sight only the curiously rounded canvas dome reminiscent of the igloo, whose shape distinguishes the Eskimo *tupek* from the pointed teepee of an Indian or the gabled tent of a white traveller. The canvas for the tops of the treeline *tupeks* is sold by the Hudson's Bay Company. Canvas was used in all the east-coast *tupeks* I have ever visited.

Treeline *tupeks* are semi-permanent. The raw log foundations are laid down in summer and are built up like cabin walls to a height of three or four feet. The snows packed around it keep out the wind, and the room inside, with rounded ceiling and floor stepping down about two feet below snow level, seems rather spacious and restful.

The Eskimos themselves, being rather little people, can move about in it freely.

Since the canvas can be replaced, the same *tupek* may serve as the winter camp of one Eskimo family for years and years. The floor matting is brushed or interlaced with spruce boughs and soon packs down smoothly. Every week or so a new carpet of fresh boughs is laid.

The old igloo tradition is closely adhered to in the internal organization of the Hudson Bay Ungava *tupek*. As in the igloo, the rear half is set aside for communal sleeping. But instead of the igloo's high rear platform made of snow, the *tupek* has a large log laid down to mark the division, the log reaching from wall to wall and providing a bench—the only furniture there is in the *tupek* to sit on. It is a peeled log as a rule, brownly polished from age and long use. The front half of the *tupek*, as also in the igloo, is devoted to the day's business —visiting, eating, storing food, singing and whatever games evolve in the long idle hours of storm. The stove is there, usually a wood-burning tin stove from the post, and the two natives *kudliaks* (the seal-oil lamps), and all the Inuk owns of kettles, tools or hunting equipment.

It seems to me a poor half-life that they lead, a life that Doutt and I, after a hasty supper with our drivers, vainly endeavoured to record that night with flashlight pictures. The picturesque spread of dull-coloured blankets that makes the great bed in the rear, the green-hued stone of the two *kudliaks*, the soft gleam, the mellow colours and textures, are destroyed in essence by the bright flashlight bulb. What charm there is in Eskimo life is not easy to put a finger on, for the reality of the Eskimo world lies almost wholly in its intangibles, things never to be found upon a naked film.

In the *tupek* that we visited, the natives watched us like friendly animals. A giggling, cross-eyed woman held a moon-faced baby to her breast. An old hag cackled with crazy laughter, pointing her fingers at us because we could not understand her language. After the first few moments of pleased surprise at the room itself, I found the *tupek* only depressing. The natives were lined up on the log like so many judges, and we squatted along the wall on our haunches to be looked at. A shy little girl — not stupid-looking, perhaps, if she had closed her mouth —sat at our very feet completely bewildered, with jaw hanging, and never took her eyes away. The crippled boy alone smiled gently, although he was watching us whenever we looked at him.

The *tupek* was just as I had expected, but was unexpectedly affecting. Was there any heigh-ho at all in the Hudson Bay country, I wondered. If so, why did I always pass it over? All the *tupeks* were much the same, the homes of a people rapidly becoming homeless, belonging scarcely more to the Northlands than we do. Certainly as a race, the Ungava Eskimo was no longer *begging to take it*. . . .

Back in our own tent that night, Mikiuk the cake-eater took our candle and tied it tightly upright to one end of a long stick, and rammed the stick down deep into the packed snow floor, making our light neat, bright and secure.

Richmond Gulf with its famous Hazard is in many ways dangerous territory. Its cliffs are sheer and it is strewn with islands among which it is difficult, either in summer or winter, not to get lost. The wise traveller stays up out of it at any season; we kept to the perilous banks lying south of the Gulf. The south banks are strictly transition territory, from the last of the bush to the true barren land —a no-man's country between Hudsonian zone and the Northern tundra. Many patches of pure rock or mossy true tundra lay exposed on the heights by the scourging of the wind, but down at water level, where Cairn Island lay, there was a fine forest.

Our last days on the Bay hit us hard. There we met our first blast, not a drifter but a steady and almost unbearable wind, drumming in our ears like the roar of a sea until we could hear nothing else. Our legs grew wind-burned because we had not put on overalls soon enough. The day following, when the thickest snow came, it packed the air like a fog around us, so blinding that we could scarcely keep track of one another. It tortured our minds for eighteen miles, and left us at sundown not only chafed all over, but with our feet badly blistered. The blisters came from a change to new socks. Only old socks that have been softened by much washing are fit for wear on a long walk in soft shoes. We always paid heavily for our blunders, but bit by bit we learned.

It was five o'clock on 22 February—six days out—when we pulled, exhausted, to the top of the last ridge, and there, where the Eskimo drivers stood pointing already, we stopped and looked down. There it was—below us, quite clear even in the sunset, was Richmond Lake, and in its middle lay tree-covered Cairn Island. Beyond, the great steaming of dark open water marked the Gulf Hazard—that famous spot that "swallows quickly." The *komatik* journey was as good as over. Beyond Cairn Island lay the land of Indians. Now the sled would be replaced by toboggans and the dogs by men.

Suppertime would come strangely in Indian country, without a single yap or a whine. We would miss the sight of the dogs—the stiff curl in the tail, the ready perking of ears, the quick twinkling movements, and all those brave small things that mean that a dog, however hard-driven, is still in good healthy condition. The breathing of the dogs had laid down on the air a little trail of undulating steam hour after hour, and the instant freezing of that moisture had covered their furry shoulders with hoarfrost, which whitened more and more as time progressed and helped us to mark the passing of each day. Often, when the world seemed overpoweringly death-like, the little jiggling black dogs fighting on ahead and the floating trail of their lung-smoke, had warmed and fed our uncertain faith in the outcome of what lay ahead.

As we stood on the hilltop the day was dying quickly.

We needed daylight especially now, for we were confronted with the Great Descent. The immediate trail led down a hill so steep that even Ross back at Great Whale River had talked about it.

"The only thing you'll have to watch," he had warned us before we started, "is that hill above Richmond Gulf. Look out for *that!*"

We peered over the edge of the height and followed it with our eyes to the very bottom. A long slope would take us perhaps a third of the way. A much longer and steeper section followed. A final short but breathtaking shoot would land us at last down onto the Lake. I felt consternation, but of course never said so.

To have solid footing, we must keep as usual to the very edge of the hill, but our long *komatik* was top-heavy for a safe balance on the steep slanting of the treacherous brink. We would all walk beside and above the *komatik*, hanging for dear life onto the load lashing, to give what help we could should the sled start slipping over the edge. No-one meant to go with it, but we were all determined to prevent any such catastrophe. The natives were tense, but did not hesitate, and we gratefully left everything to them. The dogs, sensing danger, began unhappily whining. With arms taut and backs straining, we clung to the load. Inwardly, I think, *we* all whined too; that anxious, baffled, still-trying sound that the tired dogs made expressed my own feelings perfectly. At last, safely emerged from the two preliminary hazards—the first bad, the second worse—we stopped for a moment on a natural little landing to collect our courage for the final pit-like drop. While we waited, Mikiuk was preparing the "brake."

The brake on a *komatik* is a long sealskin line that is looped two or three times around the upcurved front part of the runners, and this one would be kept tight until Mikiuk chose to release it. When the weight of the load and the steepness of the plunge swept the sled irresistibly forward, Mikiuk would let go of the strap, which would

106

whip under the runners, acting as a brake. The poor dogs would have to look out for themselves.

For a few minutes we strayed with the sled, our heels ploughing swift furrows, legs stiffened, bodies taut. But the drop was too straight. We choked in the whirl of snow that rose around us in a stifling cloud. Then Mikiuk dropped the line and we let the sled go. Over the brake and against all opposition, the *komatik* tore down the slope and made for the bottom. We slid down on numb heels not very far behind. The men were soundless, but through the maelstrom of white I heard the terrified yapping and yelping of the animals. But once the sled was at the bottom and resting on the level, the dogs seemed almost instantly recovered. None had been hurt. Some sat down eagerly panting and watched us come, sprawling. Some lay down at once as if to sleep, and others shook themselves off and friskily wagged their tails, looking proud and pleased.

We stood thankfully on the surface of Richmond Lake. Not far away, as it seemed in the clear light of early evening, lay Cairn Island with George and Boyshish waiting at the outpost.

Doutt and I, excited and in a hurry, decided to desert the tired dogs and the *komatik* party and to find our own way across the ice to the island. George's light, we thought, would be shining by now from the outpost windows to direct our path. At first, without the soft, familiar whoofing sound of the sled, the utter stillness and the gentle half-dark seemed very beautiful, but soon those landmarks that we had so confidently travelled by lost their sharp character and gradually dissolved into the purple mysteries of a world abandoned to winter. We went on walking, talking with purposeful cheer about George and Boyshish and tomorrow. The sky seemed very large and close, the dark steel of it strewn with millions of the incredible Northern stars.

At last a light stared at us unblinkingly from over a low hill and at its source we found George and Boyshish and the Hudson's Bay Company outpost. George had spent all his life on the Bay coast of Ungava, yet he could hardly wait to tell us the news. "Gosh," he cried at once without special greetings, "just wait till you see those big Richmond Gulf Indians! Seven feet tall!"

IN THE TWO TEEPEES

Richmond Gulf outpost has no factor in residence—or did not have when we were there. It is a hideaway for supplies, a roof to protect the occasional inspector, a place in which the frightened Eskimo agent who once in a while is sent up to Richmond Gulf on Company business can barricade himself against the local Indians. The front room holds a stove, a rough table, a wall of shelves that mount up to the ceiling, a long rough bench and two crude chairs. The back room has a cot at each end of it, with a medicine chest hanging on the wall above one of them, and a big rough table standing halfway between.

It was George's business, of course, to be the first one up. On the long bare tabletop in the bedroom, he had folded our two caribou robes and then thrown his own bedding down over that, making his own bed. When I waked, I saw that he was already reaching out an exploring hand to find his pants. One underweared leg at a time, George thrust himself out from under the covers and pulled his pants on. With his hair so close-cropped that no tousling was possible, he looked ready to go from the moment he slid off his bed.

"Get up, you fellows! Breakfast is ready!" he shouted, springing to his feet and swiftly pulling on his house moccasins. The stove in the front room was soon roaring and breakfast bubbled as we dressed. On this first morning with George, we indulged in a little precious coffee and happily revelled in the luxurious smell.

I examined the contents of the medicine shelves that had hung above my head as I slept. Despite months, perhaps years, of lying around open and untouched, the material seemed clean and fresh. I was curious to know with what aids the former marooned manager had provided himself: gauze bandages (opened), a bottle of calomel, several bottles of brown-pill laxatives (doubt-less to give to the Indians), two big bottles of iodine, two little bottles of mercurochrome, a big tin can of Epsom salts, some large rolls of bandaging, a bottle of aspirin tablets and some amber-coloured fluid in a clear glass bottle labelled "painkiller." I rubbed my finger over the bottles, but there was no sign of dust there.

"Grub!" shouted George impatiently as we straggled into the front room where Boyshish and he waited. What a holiday the whole thing seemed to be for Ross' young Indian helper from the post, a thin-faced, black-eyed, very bright boy of sixteen. "He needs to learn what it's all about," Ross had said, when urging us to take Boyshish. We stood around the hot stove, plates in hand, full coffee-cups steaming beside us on the table, with Boyshish and George finishing some ptarmigan that they had saved from yesterday. I could have enjoyed a little of it myself. Together with the odour of the boiling coffee it made a wonderful fragrance.

George began to give us the lowdown on the Indians. Only four had promised to go! It was, moreover, a twenty-day trip to the Upper Seal Lake region. Twenty days! We were aghast. Forty days for the trail alone was out of the question. We could never make the crossing to the Belchers if we were not back from the interior within, at most, 35 days. And how could we hope to locate and procure a seal immediately after we had reaced our objective?

The Indians suggested that we try to go to Lower Seal Lake instead of Upper. We were now north of the Seal Lakes region and Lower Seal Lake is actually north of the Upper. (Evidently the Lakes were named by the most northerly people.) It was also more likely, the Indians insisted, that we should find seals in Lower Seal Lake than in the other one, but when we pressed them for their reasons, they plainly hadn't any. George's gossip nearly ruined our good breakfast.

Before we finished eating, four of the great rawboned, strapping Indians had come in to see us. Two were at least 6' 4", and one of them was Luk Cashe, George's giant "seven feet tall!" Certainly he towered over the rest of us. We took one look at his great swinging arms and heavy shoulders, at his long spidery legs and big hands and feet, and thinking of the hard days and the dragging of toboggans, we determined to persuade Luk, at least, to come along. None of the Indians were happy at the prospect of the journey inland.

"They say yes," explained George anxiously, "but they may not go." Luk Cashe's sister was very sick, so sick that all the Indians in the place were sorrowful. It was the illness, not the journey to Seal Lakes, that our visitors wanted to talk about. Doutt had an idea.

"Get them to take us to the sick girl," he told George decisively. "I think we can help her."

We left right after breakfast for the settlement of teepees about three quarters of a mile away. Although the Indians were just taking it easy, as George boasted, the rest of us had to struggle to keep near. They shoved along ahead, the colourful tassels (whose hue depends upon the family colour—some were red, some red and white, some green) of their moccasins bobbing, their great wide shoulders in dirty white parkas lunging rhythmically from side to side. The sky was clear, and straggling trees, with snow-weighted branches gently blowing, spilled misty snow into the air. The day looked almost springlike, but the air was wet and the cold sharp in our faces.

The Richmond Gulf settlement was a poor thing. One large double teepee and one single teepee, constructed of odd pieces of canvas sewed together and hung about a central pole (a stripped and growing tree), made up the entire village. The canvas of both teepees had been burned into a stipple of little brown holes and was spotty with patches.

The great double teepee belonged to our guide, Daniel Petacumeshcum, and held Daniel and all his relations. It was in Luk Cashe's house, the little single teepee, that the sick girl lay. There on a spot ten feet in diameter, Luk's wife, their four children, an old man who may have been Luk's father, the sick sister and the giant hunter himself, all sat the long winter evenings away. Like the Eskimo *tupek*, an Ungava teepee is built on a foundation of logs with a top of canvas. But the domed shape of a *tupek* looks wind-proofed and cozy, while the pointed frame of the teepee, with naked sticks protruding in the centre, looks cold and flimsy. Like the lemmings and ptarmigan, the Ungava Indians seem to have sought shelter only in snowdrifts and burrows.

In response to his tapping, the doorflap of Luk's teepee was quickly untied and held back to admit us. We crawled in half-doubled, adding further confusion to the unbelievable crowding within. Huddled about the roaring stove in the centre was a chaotic jumble of people and objects. The stifling air, as pulsing waves from the stove met our cold skins, beat upon us full of odours strangely sickening and indefinable. No-one waiting there moved or said a word. Silent, sad and motionless, many Indians crouched or sat against the log walls on scorched dirty-grey blankets, their dark eyes shining out of their dark faces for all the world like a waiting ring of animals. Flecks of white were scattered about, feathers of ptarmigan probably plucked for last night's supper.

We had to use care not to step upon the sick girl for she lay sprawled across the floor on a dark pile of rags under our very feet. Her head was near the wall, her feet almost touching the red-hot stove. She was a pathetic sight, with stringy black hair badly matted, her dark skin very oily, her knotted hands limp upon the coarse tatters that covered her, her mouth half-open, her breathing spasmodic and laboured. The Indians, already

111

convinced that she would die, seemed suspicious but unresentful as we knelt beside her to take her pulse and her temperature.

The drying-rack was suspended from the ceiling. Mitts, socks, moccasins soaked from long use in the snow, and a suit of soggy post underwear hung from the long smooth stick. The ragged canvas admitted pale, dusky daylight and a rosy glow came from the sides of the red-hot stove. The floor had been well laid with spruce-bough matting, and although the place was hot, close, ill-smelling and filthy, I felt the sombre unity of it — the rich, earthy colourings of grey, black, copper and faded green, the knotty mottled texture of everything. I was reminded, as I looked at the scene, flecked with ptarmigan feathers, of an old piece of good tweed.

The woman's temperature was almost normal, but her pulse was extremely weak. For eight days she had not had an elimination. Just before that she had gorged herself on some flour that one of the hunters brought from Great Whale River; the flour had been mixed into the usual paste and fried hurriedly in seal grease, then eaten half-raw. She had consumed it in quantities. This is a common Indian mixture, but I doubt that a doctor would recommend it. We too expected the woman to die.

Taking a chance, we gave her a cathartic and told the Indians to keep us posted on her condition, and we escaped from the teepee none too soon, for the heat, the smells and our close proximity to the sick woman on the floor had been almost too much for us.

As we went home, George was making fun of Boyshish, and Boyshish, though shamefaced, was taking it mildly. For this expedition, Ross had let Boyshish have a blanket on credit from the post. To an Indian boy his first blanket is highly important, signifying, as it were, his ripeness for responsibility, his coming of age. Luk Cashe, on their first night at Richmond Gulf Outpost, had seen the light that George and Boyshish made in the outpost windows and had paid them a visit. It was a raw, windy night, and Luk, having stewed by the fire all evening, was ill-prepared to trek back to the settlement. His last resolution to go home faded when he caught sight of Boyshish's blanket.

"Oh!" decided Luk, petting the soft blanket like an excited child, "we are going to sleep well tonight!" And the timid young Boyshish, for Luk to him was like an ogre, put up no objection to sharing the luxury.

So the great Luk and the slender Boyshish had slept on the floor of the outpost-house together, with their feet wrapped and cozy pointing toward the fire, initiating the blanket. And all night young Boyshish lay helpless, unhappily smelling the scorching stink of the cloth where it touched the stove, as Luk Cashe burned out, in the beautiful blanket, the first ghastly and inevitable hole.

It seemed to me that we were scarcely at Richmond Gulf before we were gone again. We had time, however, to grow fond of an Indian boy whose parents, hunting in the inlands, had abandoned him for the winter. He hauled firewood for us. I like now to think that he knew for once what it was like to have enough food in his stomach. He was not more than six or seven, but he usually hunted out all day with a shotgun, on his little snowshoes, and found his own game; otherwise he was fed scraps like a beggar or went without eating. He was dreadfully thin. Recent storms had kept him hungry for a good deal of the time. One day, although he was only bid to do the hauling, he tried also to cut up our wood, and cut his foot instead. We took off his moccasin, washed the wound out with boiled water, and applied iodine and a bandage—to the amusement of all the other natives. We were angry with him for using the axe, but admired him immensely for wanting like a real hunter to earn his food.

One day we saw white Arctic fox tracks just east of the outpost, and suddenly there he was, running up the hill. I whistled, and he stopped and waited, silhouetted against green spruces and framed with the high slopes of snow. He watched us curiously for a moment, and then uncoiled the startled twist of his body and fled on up the hill. He stopped again at my second whistle and took another long look before he vanished into a thicket. Following to observe his habits, we found him as cunning as foxes are everywhere—backtracking, circling, watching us as we pursued him. He had moved slowly, however, through the thicket, as if merely baffled rather than afraid.

The Indians set a trap the next day near the shore beyond the Big Teepee and used up their best invectives, for he had eaten all the rawhide webbing out of two of our native helpers' snowshoes. It worried us, too, for now those two men would have to stay behind in the settlement until their snowshoes could be repaired!

I made every minute of the fine weather count, chasing birds and animals. Every day the natives killed rock and willow ptarmigan, which seemed endlessly plentiful. At Richmond Gulf a man need only be an expert shot and have an inexhaustible supply of ammunition in order to live a normal winter through. (It is the lack of shells, not the lack of wild life, which accounts for the not-infrequent starvation of the treeline Indians, I eventually decided.)[11] I was constantly on snowshoes, which, when hunting birds, is a maddening situation, especially with the narrow, poorly balanced snowshoes that we had brought from Moosonee. Birds fly into the woods when startled. There the snow, protected from wind, is softest and deepest, and there I often floundered about. It was not the discomfort that I most hated, but the unseizable opportunities. On 1 March I heard a hairy woodpecker, which I should have collected, but it was on a steep, snowdrifted hillside and I could not even get near enough to see it. But on 2 March I had the luck near evening to step right in among some bedded willow ptarmigan. It was very early dusk, but the ptarmigan were already sleeping and only flew up when I actually landed in the midst of the night-forms. There they were, each in his tiny hole in the snowbank, very near a willow thicket on which to browse the first thing in the morning. To find the forms actually occupied afforded me a rare sight. The Indians kept telling George about an owl that was the size of a jay, and about some other large dark-coloured bird that frequented the settlement, but I could find neither. Of the birds wintering in the inland, they knew nothing.

Unlike the house at Great Whale River, the little outpost at Richmond Gulf never seemed like home. But with the white hills, as always, and with the still, green forests, I quickly felt familiar and at peace. And as always at the leaving, I suffered that faint twinge of sadness. Farewell to that now well-packed path, with the great broken rock marking the turning up over the hill . . . to the bashed-in pail of garbage where the Whisky Jacks were sure to come . . . once again, farewell!

Our leavetaking was ceremonious and very slow. Old Man Petacumeshcum sat at the head of the Big Teepee with a great pile of fresh wood shavings lying in creamy curls around him. He had been whittling out a snow-spoon for us as a parting gift. It was at least four feet long, made like a great ladle all of one piece. He was a very dark, wild-faced, long-haired ancient, decrepit in his limbs, but very skilful with the crooked knife. An Indian depends for almost all his accomplishments in manu-facture upon the crooked knife. Old Man Petacumesh-cum, pulling the knife always toward him, shaved the snowspoon down as smoothly as if he had had a plane. He seemed anxious to make a really good spoon, to show his gratitude for the food we were leaving, George said, and to make things on the trail as easy as possible for his son Daniel who would be our foreman. It was a splendid spoon, carved out of a spruce tree, the lightest available wood at Richmond Gulf. The other Indians looked at it with admiration and handled it reverently. We used it later for almost two weeks on the trail, until someone let Luk Cashe do the shovelling. Luk hooked it too deeply

115

into a drift, and instead of pulling it out and sinking it more shallowly, as any other man would do, he just lifted up on it, breaking it into two pieces. The other men were so angry that Jacob Rupert the peacemaker carved out a new spoon one night when he should have been sleeping — using a spruce log almost seven inches in diameter.

We had visited the Big Teepee once before, with its two stoves and the hanging curtain dividing the space into two separate family compartments. Daniel had a daughter of fifteen, wiry, quick and pretty, and a son of seventeen who was light-skinned and very frail. Daniel's squaw was fat and a very fast talker—"a meat-axe type of woman," George translated as the local verdict, "and very hard to get along with." Thomas George lived in the Big Teepee also, with his shy, young wife, as did Daniel's other brother and the Two Old People. At our first visit to the double teepee, George had explained that Daniel felt that he had something that we really ought to see. It was a rickety old gramophone, given to the household by a white adventurer many years ago. The natives had all been silent, with the exception of Daniel, who talked all the time and smiled incessantly, trying to make us feel comfortable. He was the centre of all eyes on that visit. Finally he had opened up the gramophone. At the first sound of it the faces all changed. If not on the lips, smiles were at least in the eyes of everybody. The gramophone was, no doubt, Daniel's way of paying us his very highest honour.

The next night after our introduction to the teepees, all the hunters came down to visit the outpost, bringing the gramophone with them. I knew then that I had never before seen an Indian when he was happy. Daniel and his son had a perpetual contest to do the playing. The records were Irish jigs mostly, many with lyrics, and although they couldn't understand a word of the English, the natives listened eagerly and smiled often without special reason. I was terrified once when Luk Cashe reached over to pick up the favourite, "Turkey in the

Straw." (It had already been broken once and was mended with adhesive tape.) But Daniel's hand intercepted and kept Luk away.

On the morning of our departure the Indians were all silent. Indeed they were very sad. Luk Cashe's sister, the sick girl of the single teepee, had been well on the road to recovery, but had gorged again in the night on seal grease and flour and was again stricken. This time, they all told George gravely, she would be *sure* to die. Distracted, we had called on her with the cathartic and with a sober warning that she must stay for some time on a strictly liquid diet, but we felt pretty hopeless after the visit.

The Big Teepee was filled with a press of people, both local and visiting. Three new Indians had joined us on Saturday—Jimmy Sandy and the two Ruperts, who actually lived on the way to the Seal Lakes. It was plainly our good luck to have them. Jacob Rupert was very young, but he had an intelligent face of unusual gentleness and he wore the official cap of the Hudson's Bay Company "Good Hunter," with the shining metal insignia of the Company on its front. This is a distinction not easily to be won in Ungava, the land of good hunters, and it became evident early on the trail that Daniel Petacumeshcum was exceedingly jealous of Jacob Rupert—of the "Good Hunter" cap, probably. Both the Ruperts were painfully neat, putting our other hunter slovens to shame. In this also, however, Daniel was a personal competitor, for he, of all the Richmond Gulf crew, was touched with a desire for elegance, colour and ceremony in his daily life.

Because Eskimos are reputed to be the best hunters of the seal, Doutt had persuaded the little Eskimo Ekumiak to go inland with us. Ekumiak had made a fine four-day race to his own winter camp and back again to the outpost. He had brought along, also to go inland, one old seal-hunting Husky dog. On the trail, to the great chagrin of our white guide George, he and Ekumiak and the old Husky dog were hitched all three to one trace and all pulled one toboggan together.

117

Ekumiak was better dressed than the Indians. He wore good English wool pants, an almost new canvas parka, and he had a seal *(netchek)* bag, made with a flap like a knapsack, for carrying his personal belongings. He wore a billed wool cap, without any insignia, and had fine hairy-leg *komiks* with bottoms of thick square-flipper seal. His boots were bleached to a creamy colour with urine—the only efficient way the natives have for bleaching Northern skins. Ekumiak carried a pipe and always smoked during the rests, at lunch, and even sometimes in our tent in the evening.

Both Daniel and Jacob Rupert wore white handkerchiefs tied around their heads to protect their ears from the cold. The ends of the heavy muslin were tied together in the front, the knot hidden in the fold of the cap where the bill and the crown were snapped. The bandage effect seemed to me ludicrous, but evidently it did not seem so to the Indians.

My companion and I were not too satisfied with our own outfits. We wore berets under the hoods of our packas to escape the consciousness of hair that was always tousled. The Indians are more practical; they clip their hair almost all off. Our fine-textured parkas so lightweight and warm, were actually inferior to the cheap canvas parkas of the Indians, for ours were highly inflammable and would blaze up at a spark, nor were they sufficiently porous for the active life on the trail. To be sure, our tan-coloured cloth looked clean long after it wasn't, while the Indians in all-white parkas were obviously always dirty. The natty Ruperts were, of course, cleaner than others.

There was but little colour left in the Indians' costumes, considering that Indian life was once so full of it. The Rupert boys had red braid around the bottoms of their parkas, and every Indian face was circled in the narrow strip of brown dog fur common to native hoods in Ungava, and every moccasin drawstring had a coloured tassel-end flopping—little red and white brushes swinging with every step. Daniel Petacumeshcum had a braid-trimmed rifle bag tied on the very top of his own toboggan, a few coloured tassels outlined the bearpaw snowshoes at the points, but these bits of gaiety were lost in the general impression of drabness.

There were seven toboggans ready to go. Daniel and Thomas George could not start off when the rest of us did; it was they who had allowed the fox to eat out their snowshoe webbings. The supply of caribou thongs is greatly limited nowadays, and no-one at Richmond Gulf ever owned extra snowshoes. The two hunters promised to catch up with us on their new shoes by Tuesday.

Our party made quite a picture. Luk Cashe had the worst load—the stoves, the canned meat, all the heavy pieces, more than 200 pounds. The others had connived to put it over on Luk. He had no notion that he was treated unfairly. Like the big brute that he was, he stepped into the circle of his sealskin line as it lay opened on the snow, and picked the line up and set it across his chest and without a grunt or a stumble started off. He had no idea what was dragging behind him, but silently lunged along following the others. His own name, Luk Cashe, means "Luke the Ugly," but the name that the Indians used most often meant "the Tearer" — because Luk was always wrecking something.

An Indian toboggan in Ungava is distinguished by narrowness and the flexibility of the bottom. Not more than sixteen inches of width accommodates the load, which is distributed very low and evenly to keep the toboggan from tipping over. It is usually about twelve feet long and made of tamarack, a very strong wood. Planed down with a crooked knife to a quarter-inch thickness, the two long bottom boards are pointed at the rear and steamed and curled up in front, and then are joined by five or six thick and narrow struts that are lashed onto the bottom boards by thongs. The thongs are countersunk beneath the runners. The load is packed into bags not more than three feet long or fifteen inches high, in order to fit well between the struts. Through loops provided at the ends of each strut, a single long thong is run, making a guy-line to tie any lashings to. A piece of canvas covers the whole and lashing lines tightly secure it.

It is a common sight, when Richmond Gulf Indians prepare for the trail, to see them peeling slim saplings, straight sticks about four feet in length, with which to float themselves as they stride dancingly along on their great round bearpaw snowshoes. The pulling line on a toboggan is a thong of caribou, and the strain of the pull comes chiefly on the chest. Only Daniel Petacumeshcum shifted his position much. He used to lower his chest-thong occasionally to waist level, and then insert his fists between the line and his stomach. He was shrewdly progressive; unlike the more primitive of the natives, he never bothered to carry a dancing-stick; but I liked best to watch the men with the saplings.

What solemnity and kissing there was in the Big Teepee! All the relatives from far and near were sitting or squatting in the tent by the time we came. Thomas George's wife, who was soon to have a baby, followed him about and whispered to him while he loaded up his box of shells. The Indians would be hunting their own meat, they had decided, as always on the winter trail. It seemed a dubious plan to us, but that was the way the men wanted it, Daniel said shortly, and it permitted a very important reduction of our essential load. Thomas George was first to leave, kissing first his own wife and his own child, and then on around the circle kissing every relative, even those by marriage; and each was kissed twice, first on the cheek or forehead and then on the crown of the head. With the few people present who were not relatives, he shook hands very solemnly. All the hunters who were to go with us did likewise. And on all sides there were tears and distracted faces as if these were indeed their last farewells. They were a sad lot—a fearful and darkly melancholy people, in a land where life even at best is uncertain.

120

The morning was half-gone before we could finally gather about our loaded toboggans. The long thin lines by which the toboggans were to be pulled lay carefully spread out in open circles upon the snow, so that each man, even in his great round snowshoes, could step within, lift the line up to rest across his chest, and, with a surging lunge of his body and a great outward swing of his leg, be off and away.

In a moment or two after we had all assembled, the trail-breaker, with his difficult path and lighter load, started off. But the rest of us stopped to listen to the shouting of the natives at the shore-line. We ran to see the fine white Arctic fox—the same no doubt that I had whistled to yesterday behind the outpost, the same beauty that had fled yesterday so much alive up the long hill. He was trapped now by his hind legs, and he lay crouched and vicious, his ears back, his eyes shining, his long teeth bared. I took a picture of him there regretfully. He would make a distinguished pelt, and he had caused us a great deal of trouble by eating the webbing out of the snowshoes, but snowshoes, I couldn't help reflecting, ought to be left up in a tree. For foxes as well as people life in Ungava is very uncertain.

THE DANCE OF THE BEARPAW SNOWSHOES

From the Big Teepee we followed the eastern shoreline of Cairn Island, cutting across the long northeast arm of the island and, after about two hours' walking, dropping down onto the frozen Gulf. We were heading east by south.

While crossing the island, the Indians kept to the trail, the trail-breaker (carrying only about a hundred pounds) going ahead and packing down the snow. Except on this first morning, when he was not with us, Daniel Peta-cumeshcum would be the trail-breaker, Doutt and I, without toboggans, going immediately behind. When several toboggans had already smoothed it out, the trail

would not be too difficult for the short-legged Ekumiak
with George and the old Husky dog. They pulled all the
noon supplies, the cooking outfit and the lunch grub. The
dog was leashed out in front 25 feet from the toboggan,
to make him think he was pulling at his own Eskimo sled.
Ekumiak was hitched to the dog's leash some ten feet
back of the Husky. George had a separate leash about six
feet long. Going downhill, Doutt and I sometimes had a
little fun by jumping onto their toboggan and riding.

The Indians usually wore the taut line like a piece of
chest harness, but they did vary their dancing according
to the terrain. On rough bumpy ground, some walked
with their arms down and back, their hands clasping the
lines behind them, to ease the strain of the load. But when
the going was smooth, they seldom touched rope. The
men who carried saplings grasped them at either end,
and, with elbows rigid and in perfect rhythm, swung their
arms freely from side to side and from side to side,
swinging so regularly that if I were very near them it was
almost impossible for me not to fall into sleep. That
would never do, for as Ross says, "I've seen those inlanders take a yard between strides"—a thing few people on
snowshoes are up to. Doutt and I are both six-footers, but
we took no yard between strides. Yet if we hadn't been
able to take more steps per minute than the Indians took
we could never have kept up with them, and if short-
legged Ekumiak hadn't been able to take more steps per
minute than we could manage and about twice as many as
the poorest walker among the Indians, he would not have
stayed with the party either.

Puffing, wordless, almost running, Ekumiak kept up
somehow. And the old dog! Puzzled no doubt to be
pulling such a strange thing and with such companions,
he was silent, cowed, completely obedient. He did not
look any too fit; his tail was not in a very stiff curl nor
were his ears very sharply pointing, but he wasn't sick.
He shook himself off brightly enough whenever he fell
into a snowdrift, and he wolfed down his seal grease and

122

oatmeal at noontime like any healthy, half-starved Husky. He was just a little old and quite a little worn, but very willing—like his master.

On we went across the broken silvery slopes, the Indians swinging their legs outward in wide and difficult curves, almost half-circles, for with the spreading pan-shaped bearpaws their shoes would have knocked together badly otherwise. Even as it was, the wooden edges were clicking a good deal by sunset, when legs grew weary and hip action was half-hearted. Often in late hours the click and clack of wood on wood could be heard like an obligato accompanying evening. It was a pleasant sound—a sort of North Ungava version of castanets.

The long slim snowshoes Doutt and I had brought from Moose Factory were far less efficient in the deep snow than were the Gulf Indians' great round bearpaws, but were more natural for the unskilful to walk on. There were no extra bearpaws to be had, moreover, which left no choice for us. In our shoes we could stride almost straight ahead, but our narrow toes were very apt to get snow-loaded.

Taut across their straining breasts, the dark thong pulled and sawed on the bodies of the Indians the live-long day. With almost 200 pounds of dragging load behind them and more than a little friction from icy hummocks, the Indians often pressed their huge dark hands to their sore chests at night, bruised and muttering, and squinted their swelling eyelids together over burning and bloodshot eyes, half-sick from a hard day's journey. Yet even so, we seemed never able to move fast enough. . . . Steadily we fell back, an hour, a day, two days, finally a week behind the Indians' own estimated schedule, while spring, with a bird-note here, a little open water there, a few minutes more of visible sun, a barely perceptible melting and sinking underneath our feet, was pressing steadily upon us. And each day lost meant another day paid for—a further dwindling of our scant resources.

It was a costly seal that we hunted, and the cost seemed heavy indeed to me, for on the Belchers we could spend only whatever money might be left over. Everything in the Far North is expensive except labour, but when food, fuel and ammunition are provided the cost of labour soars. With gasoline on the Belchers at $1.50 per gallon and an ancient fuel-eating motor in some old island boat, we could not hope for much scouting during the summer. To be too poor to range freely, once we had come to the Belchers, would be heartbreaking! But so things were. Our little seal was neither as easy nor as cheap to take as we had expected. That was all there was to it.

That we might spend all our money and still not find *kasagea* was something that Doutt and I never mentioned. But always in the dim recesses of my consciousness hovered a thin cloud of dread, growing large or sinking almost into nothing according to our luck and the weather.

At the start, on the Gulf ice with no hills to climb, we made good time, keeping our compass first toward a point on the far mainland near the mouth of the Wiachuan River. At that spot we should start inland, eventually to join Clearwater River. Clearwater River has its source in Clearwater Lake, but strong currents near the mouth keep its water open. For many days we would climb up and around those deep-rushing rapids. Every river in Ungava springs from inland heights and plunges to sea level with crashing falls. The larger the river, the less likely to be frozen. There was another river, unnamed, which somewhat paralleled Clearwater River, but was a good deal smaller, and this was the unmapped road on which the Richmond Gulf Indians usually travelled into the Seal Lakes region. Eventually in the interior, where all rivers are shallower and more thickly frozen, we planned to cut overland and find Clearwater River again.

Just opposite the mouth of Wiachuan River and only a

few miles from the mainland lay the island that was our first day's objective. We reached it about five in the afternoon. "Too late," said George apprehensively, looking at his watch. "Too dark to be making camp!"

With Daniel absent, the Indians were leaderless. They came straggling across the Gulf ice wearily, but still dancing, swinging the cradled sticks before them, rolling their shoulders from side to side, from side to side, feeling no doubt as tired soldiers do marching to music. Perhaps like music, the rhythm of the swinging sticks keeps the Indians from feeling their exhaustion.

The islands loomed above us—a towering rockland, every brown cleft silted with snow. Luckily for us, the island was divided by an enormous cut right down the middle. It was now a snow-filled and spruce-wooded valley. Clumps of trees stood on the narrow valley floor and the sharp slopes on either side were crowded with green. On the trees were the ferniest branches that we had seen for some time, rescued from the winds by the gorge-like depths of the shelter. The sky was pinkish lavender, the light grey and the still air numbingly cold.

Shouting loudly and with many motions, the Indians quickly chose the campsite. Ekumiak and the old dog stuck close to Doutt or me. As the day had progressed, I had been amazed by Ekumiak. Like Alice in Wonderland he had seemed gradually to be growing smaller. I had known, of course, that the strength and size of the Indians depressed him, wounding his natural ego. The high spirits, the ready humour, the cheerful self-reliance so characteristic of him on the *komatik* journey from Great Whale River, were all gone. He was obviously miserable and seemed curiously out of place for a man who was travelling in his native country. It was, however, a rather bad journey for a stoutish fellow of 50, on foot and with but one old dog. He would be of little use for trail duties, but he did what he could by keeping out of the way.

One with the snowspoon and one with a snowshoe,

125

two Indians shovelled out a depression a little larger than our tent floor and about eighteen inches deep. Axes boomed against the frozen tree trunks, the sound echoing and re-echoing through the valley. The trees fell with sharp crack but no thud, the snow mist faintly rising all over the ground. At the tent site, the two shovelling Indians were trampling down the floor of the circle first with one foot and then the other. Some dragged whole trees to the trampled place and lopped off the branches on the spot. Some lopped the branches where the tree fell, and carried green fronds by the armful to the tent site. Starting at the rear and moving swiftly forward, the floor-maker began overlapping and interweaving the boughs into a springy, green, over-all carpet. The tent stretchers grabbed up the canvas, unrolled it carefully over the bushy circle, and tied the tent ridge onto the ridgepole. The crossed shears for front and back were now raised and the ridgepole ends were lashed onto the top of them. Next the guy-ropes at the tent corners were stretched tight and tied to the four spruce poles, pegged some four feet down into the snow. The remaining guy-ropes were now fastened in the same way. The snow-cloth, or sod-cloth—a canvas strip always sewed completely around the bottom of any Northern tent—was pulled well out and banked heavily with snow. Our floor tarpaulin was thrown over the boughs in the rear half of our tent where we should be sleeping. In the front half the woven boughs lay exposed. Our tin stove rested upon four pegs near the door, clearing the floor by about six inches, and the stovepipe was rammed through the asbestos-lined hole—also provided in any Northern tent. All was motion and sound and hurry.

Luk Cashe was the champion chopper, and was seldom allowed to do anything but chop. With wild abandon he threw his axe into the very hearts of trees at the first blow. When he stripped branches off, he turned the felled tree upside down and with one stroke dropped ten or twelve branches. They floated noiseless and green

126

from his hand, like leaves, in rapid succession. When Luk finished with a tree, he had a good clean pole, five of which were needed for each tent.

The spruce branches were piled up in heaps of fragrant tatters, the canvas unrolled with a shout and a heave. The stovepipe near the door stuck out menacingly at an ugly angle, as it always does from any tent or teepee or *tupek* in Ungava. The stovepipe is as much a part of the east shore as the Bay is. Few people, even among the natives, would try to get through a winter without it. After two days in that rimy air, our new black stovepipe had been thoroughly rusted, and now it looked as if we had used it for years.

It was at camp building and at camp tearing down that the Indians did most of their talking. In harsh deep voices they spilled out volleys of words, seeming half the time to be speaking to themselves, for they never stopped their agitated motions or took time to turn to anyone in particular. Shouting, muttering, the white-clothed figures scurried about, seeming but voices, shoulders, booms and flashing blades. For perhaps an hour, as they raised the two tents—one for us and one for them—they flurried the silent valley with a strange transport of life.

The boom of Luk's axe was usually the last sound of nightly labour. It was well after dark when the wood-chopping stopped, with enough logs stored for both tents for the night. It is dangerous to put off camp-making until dusk, for even in the light, chopping into frozen trees is tricky business. If an axe hits a frozen tree at a slightly off-angle, it may glance fatally. Even a bullet will glance from a hard-frozen tree. The Indians by bitter experience had learned to use care in the winter with bullets and axes—all except Cashe, whom Providence had thus far protected from his own gun and whom strength protected in tree-chopping. For Luk's axe never glanced, but with the first great blow sank deep into any tree that he aimed at.

Yet no care could be taught to the Indians when their

lives were not endangered. Despite the very wide angling of the stovepipe, the good tent with which we provided them was soon peppered with great brown holes burnt by the sparks flying out from their chimney. Against all our protests they stoked the stove so violently that flames shot up from the smokestack for four feet or more and showers of fire poured out of it continuously. At any hour of the night we could look from our own tent at the beautiful leaping flames, and hear the lulling roar or the vicious crackle of their fire. For all our consternation, we soon learned to enjoy what was splendid in it, the cheerful sounds and the glow. Since we were unable to teach them any moderation in the management of their stove, we let ourselves be glad of the livid redness of it, which, although we provided them with candles, was usually their only evening light.

By the time wood for the night had been brought in, George had a fire blazing hotly in our stove and supper was ready. Before we pegged down the door-flap and prepared to eat, I took a look around. The stars were glimmering in the sky and the once ghostly valley lay purple, in dark unbroken shadows. The old dog had been fed and lay wearily sleeping just beyond the tent door. His face was completely covered by his fat warm tail, and his shaggy fur faintly rose and fell with each peaceful breath. That night, Ekumiak had murmured anxious syllables to the dog as he fed it, while we all listened, understanding nothing. Now, at any sound from the neighbouring tent, Ekumiak would appear to be profoundly disturbed. Often he went to the tent door and undid it, to peer out at the sleeping dog.

"Your dog is all right," we tried to assure him, and told George to explain that the Indians wouldn't ever hurt his *kingmee*. But Ekumiak shook his head at us sadly, sitting cross-legged in his own corner, propping his elbow on one knee and resting his chin in his hand.

"*Elizaponga*" ("I am afraid"), he answered simply.

He was afraid not only of the Indians but probably of

the journey too. It was clear that the Indians looked on him with hostility, and we were beginning to be sorry that he had come. Indians and Eskimos, George insisted, never did get along well together. The land we were in now was Indians' country.

On that first night the Indians were in holiday spirits. They talked for a long time after we were quiet, their voices loud and excited. We even heard them laughing. We should have had more relish for their laughter if we had known how seldom in the future we were to hear that sound.

A PIECE OF LICHEN

The next morning, with faces numbed and eyes burning from the cold, we followed the trail-breaker on down through the valley, 500-foot rocks rising in smooth reticence on either side. The pass that we travelled through was like the dip between a camel's humps, and the island as we looked back at it soon merged into the hilly whiteness of the whole.

All land visible in any direction was a flowing batik of rocks, spruce and snow. The pale sky left the horizon without sharp definition and the world with no limits. It brought a feeling of futility to anyone who studied it. It brought a longing to sit quietly and rest, to lose one's fretful desires and feeble ambitions in a wide nirvana of nothingness. It brought a great scorn for all petty activities and a strange willingness to accept death. A man would be unlucky to be much alone with such scenery.

Out of the valley and down on Gulf ice again, we found the snow-covered surface so firm that we could take off our snowshoes. The temporary freedom was wonderful. In less than an hour we walked the three miles and a half to the mainland. A stiff wind from the north was rising; with warning zip and twirl, it was whirling up little cyclones of ice particles from the crisply frosted surface of the Gulf. As we waited at the edge of the mainland for all toboggans to gather, the sun became fog-covered and wet rime began moving in upon us.

Ahead lay the difficult hills that we must begin to climb. They were great rock lumps, wind-cleared and barren, except for thick growths of spruce down in the gorges and crusts of grey-green reindeer lichens on the tops of the highest knolls. The lower hills were round and white and rested as if cupped within green hands, for all the countless runways of the summer water were green with slim rows of trees, pushing delicately up the sloping valley sides and tapering each to an end like extending fingers. In the moist environment at the base of the spruces there were always little willows and alders growing, from four to eight feet high. Beyond the scales of rock that usually marked the edges of the reindeer lichen, we always found andropogon, and wherever there was an open sweep not too high and rocky, there was an inevitable ground-cover of Labrador tea. What a strange thing it must seem to the Indians, I often found myself thinking, that white men should choose to come in winter to such a milkless and honeyless land.

We climbed less than a mile before we stopped to rest, and there as we rested, Daniel Petacumeshcum and Thomas George, with new webbing in their snowshoes, caught up with us. They had covered the eighteen miles that now lay between us and Richmond Gulf, since daybreak, being unhindered by a load. Their toboggans had been cached ahead for them by other hunters from the settlement two days before. We lunched, and soon after reached the ridge top, from which we could look back over our whole day-and-a-half's hard trail. The drifter had not come, or perhaps we had climbed out of it. The snow eddies were settled. We ought to have continued forward, but Daniel Petacumeshcum, who was already exhausted with his haste, now took charge of the expedition in no uncertain manner. At the next spruce woods, he decided, only a mile eastward, we must make the night's camp.

And camp we did, grateful for the forest and for the strange sight of the white hills squatting to the south of us, gigantic and very round (like great padded tea-cosies), and for the shielding cliff behind our tent, perhaps 900 feet high.

Our camp floor on this night was trampled down properly, with moccasined feet, not with snowshoes, for Daniel thought that snow trampled down with snow-shoes made a cold floor. And our spruce boughs, as Daniel dictated the laying, made a tightly woven mattress eight to ten inches high. Daniel gloried in power and in all kinds of ceremony, shaking hands with us importantly whenever he entered our tent even with a trivial question, while Ekumiak, the Eskimo, whose hand was *never* shaken, looked on with jealous and indignant eyes; when Daniel departed, Ekumiak sometimes spat upon the spruce boughs with a gesture of eloquent meaning, and made a syllable of scornful sound.

On the third morning we descended to the Wiachuan River, looking back wonderingly at the great hill that we had just crossed over. Now we could trail rapidly along on the river's frozen surface, listening often to the roar and boom of open falls. The first falls, which we had skirted overland, had been down at the mouth of the river, but the second one was ahead, and soon we could see the white mist in a spreading cloud above the rush of the stream.

The second falls on the Wiachuan River drops neatly down a 65-foot cliff. The ice, in a fixed mass of fantastic roofing, hung above the top of the falls with the pounding rush of water sweeping out from beneath it. Mist was thick in the air and the moisture seared our cheeks like steam. It was a sharp, sparkling morning, 40 degrees below zero.

The climb up out of the river was dangerous and steep,

and the deep-drifted portage around the falls threatened our toboggans with hidden rocks. Once around the falls we again descended to the river, and travelled on it for another mile before we stopped to rest. It was only ten o'clock in the morning, but we were exhausted. We all took some tea and waited for half an hour.

It was clear that we must begin leaving caches, for during the climbs the normal loads were too heavy; the men preferred, Daniel said, to make temporary deposits and return for them every night rather than to attempt too much at one time. Of what good was such niggardly advance? But of what good our consternation! It was clear, even to us, that the men pulled more than they should. Before the third afternoon was well started, the night camp was selected and another day was already over.

It was good for Doutt and me on that day that so much scientific work in Ungava still has to be done. In different directions as always, we set out exploring, forgetting our despair in excitement. For here near thickets and not far from open water, life persisted freely even in winter.

For me, the study of birds naturally combines with the study of animals. I first followed the tracks of an otter, who, although capable of hunting down ptarmigan, will usually feed on sluggish fish in winter and will never go far from open pools if he can help it. I soon found the typical track—a succession of slides with a few footprints between, where the otter had been running to gain power for the next take-off on his smooth-surfaced stomach. The track was about ten inches wide, and the animal often slid for a twelve-foot stretch at a time. He was an otter with real impetus, skating straight into snowdrifts and out on the opposite side. I never found him, but it was worth the cold blisters that broke out again, revoltingly, on my face, just to follow his clear track, and worth the frozen cheeks and the painful application with snow, just to walk at will over places where probably no other white man had ever walked, and to dispel even by a little the enshrouding mystery. Ptarmigan thickly browsed, and there were signs also of martens. But wandering-time was all too short. At four in the afternoon it was already time to look out for night-forms full of sleeping ptarmigan. It grew less cold near evening—36 below zero. The rising temperature hinted of a coming wind.

Our fourth morning's course lay on a river bottom. If it hadn't been so, we should not have done any travelling, for on the high banks above us blew a roaring gale. The sky was hazy, with dark clouds slowly drifting, and the sun had a big yellow circle around it. The temperature rose swiftly 36 to 16 below zero. But we pushed ahead, miraculously able to make headway, accidentally protected by the splendid heights of the cliffs that walled in the river. Above us the storm raged with fitful force — sometimes petulant, sometimes in downright fury—while we listened, awed, to the mournful sounds that came through gaping clefts in the rocks. The heavy moisture, always brought in by the wind, made the air excruciatingly cold.

I saw the Indians often look up at the rocky heights glooming above us, darkly threatening. The tops of the cliffs were cracked and broken by frost. Sometimes we walked among huge fragments that had fallen into the river and lay scattered ponderously about. The birds were all gone, fled into cover. Only we men and the one old dog braved the storm. We kept to our shelter, and like ghosts of the unadmitted dead still walked in the world even though we were not of it.

Once more Fortune favoured us. By noon the wind died, just before we moved out of the river. One of the Indians shot a fat ptarmigan, no doubt because the bird in an excess of gladness to be out of its shelter forgot to be wary. The temperature had risen to nine below zero. Precariously rocked by the blasts, we climbed half a mile upwards and then lunched, while Daniel Petacumeshcum stood doubtfully frowning at the very high hill ahead.

Half of our food was temporarily cached at last night's camp, a good six miles back. There would not be much more daylight. While four Indians started back for the caches, the rest of us pressed onward, but only for a mile or two before we made camp in a sheltered hillside valley. (There the Indians felled a tree that had a Canada jay's nest in it, and I found six jays out feeding that same afternoon.)

When I came in that night, Ekumiak was sitting in his own corner mending his *komik* and looking very smug. George said Ekumiak had just been boasting. He would not *always* be a trouble to us! *He* intended to be the fellow who would get the inland seal! And not *tousik* (one), but *mikiavik* (many)!

As George decribed the boast, Ekumiak's smile widened. He held up five fingers and counted them off pretentiously with his other hand. I took the opportunity to look over the things in the Eskimo's spread-out personal store. He had there everything that he used in a small post sugar-sack: a Gillette razor and some blades (Eskimos abominate whiskers), a small sewing-box (with thimble, needles, sinew, thread and a small piece of canvas for repairing his clothing), a pair of post snow-glasses, a bit of soap and a can of lighter-fluid. Except for one blanket and his hunting equipment—two harpoon shafts, one harpoon head and 30 feet of strong sealskin line—he carried nothing else. Ekumiak was of course just a spoiled east-coast "cake-eater," but the best one that I can imagine. Even his boasting was not vanity, but only a pathetic attempt to regain his self-respect, to make us glad that we had brought him, to show his gratitude for our care, and to justify himself with his own people and with his God for his great audacity. For we were gradually coming to understand that when Ekumiak came into the "inlands" he had defied a great Ungava tradition. Eskimos of the Hudson Bay coast of Ungava belong to Hudson Bay and to the shores of salt water. To the Indians belong all the land.

The wind next morning was fearful. Gloomy and anxious we remained at the camp. A few of the Indians, in the very face of the drifter, moved some caches ahead by a half-day's journey and returned that night to our camp. Daniel Petacumeshcum tried to hunt for the men who made caches, but although he stayed out for several hours he killed only ten ptarmigan. Since a ptarmigan is scarcely larger than a pigeon, it was not enough.

The wind insanely swept over the hill-ridge looming above us, pushing the snow off in swoops onto our tents. We all assumed there was a blizzard in progress, until I climbed some of the lower hills hoping for bird signs, and discovered that no snow was falling. It was all being swept up off the ground. Soft and wet and six feet deep under the spruces, it piled up heavily on the toes of my snowshoes and I took many a spill and would be nearly smothered by the time I could tunnel out. I was soon cold, bruised and miserable. I found no bird and no sign of a bird. Once more in the tent, I pulled my body together with a little mending of clothes and pulled my mind together with a Husky lesson from Ekumiak.

That night (our fifth inland), at the evening conerence that we always had with Daniel (George interpreting), Doutt and I were depressed beyond measure. At least another week, Daniel said, with the load that we carried, was between us and Lower Seal Lake. The men, moreover, must have more time for the *towhoon*, meaning hunting. They needed more, much more, of the meat of the white bird! To allow for the *towhoon*, we must all go more slowly or stop and camp earlier in the evenings.

Yet not all of Daniel's news that night was depressing. Soon, he said, we should leave this coastal country, known as the valley of the rivers, and would enter higher, terraced country called the land of the lakes. Upon the terraces of the hilltop plateaus, lakes would lie in long chains, almost joined to one another, and would make a continuous region of frozen water up and down the slopes, so that our progress would be smoother than it had ever been and much faster. These chains of lakes would lead into Clearwater River; that river would lead into Clearwater Lake, which leads directly into Lower Seal Lake—and so to the end of our rainbow!

By March the fifth, we entered the Land of the Lakes. There the first bird that I saw was carrying a mossy bit of greenness. Strange that a little thing could mean so much—just the sight of a Canada jay flying off with a piece of lichen in its bill. I tried to forget the sight, but couldn't, naturally, for to me it meant nest-building. An early spring! Swiftly softening and flooding water and the break-up of the ice bridge to Tukarak.

I saw the jay on the first lake that we crossed in the inland uplands. The uplands were a mild-featured region of low, barren, rocky, rounded hills, where slender lakes went stepping down in terraces to the valleys below. We crossed six lakes on the first day's march and four more of them the day after. Actually we had already been over the divide. Day by day, now, were we gradually descending. Seeing always below us the sweep of terrace upon terrace like steps going down the hills, we seemed on top of the world. The heavy white clouds (which Ekumiak called *nevoors*), rolling against the watery greyness of sky, seemed so close that we were almost in them. As we pushed across the terraced country, I began to feel the mounting triumphal surge of the strange journey, a swifter beating of the heart as we moved farther and farther inland, an increasing excitement as the world about us grew more sweeping in its vistas, more raw and barren and wide. The hills that we climbed between the fifth and the eighth of March had fewer and fewer shrubs, and strewn across their tops lay huge spectacular boulders, grey, heroic in effect and primitive. It was a country for greatness of every sort.

Ekumiak again was cowering like his old dog, and I tried to look about me with his eyes, to see the earth in all

136

its strangeness, and tried to realize what a Bay-trained Eskimo must feel in the forbidden virgin mountains of the Indians' land.

We started with propitious weather on our first day among the lakes. From a gritting cold in the morning (although the temperature read only three below zero), the day grew swiftly more fair, and the wind dropped, with scarcely a breeze left. The Canada jay with his piece of lichen would certainly be happy in such a sun, but despite the glory of the sky I was half miserable at the sudden brightness.

Not far below the barren wind-swept heights of the terraced hilltops, there were bush-like spruces, which sprawled in streaks along every valley and followed in thin clear pencilled margins the outline of each long lake; but no alder or willow bushes were found in terraced regions. We continued to camp at night among scrubby little trees. On the higher slopes, trees were wind-twisted and pressed down into a kind of vine, but in the deeper valleys they grew as much as twenty feet tall, and, strangely enough, tamaracks began to appear among the spruces in the swampiest regions, always singly, however, never in groves or clusters. Occasionally, wind-whipped and scanty but still upright and tall, one would find a good-sized tamarack tree right out in the open, withstanding all storms. In one camp we burned tamarack logs as thick as the arm.

We had said goodbye, when we left the region of the deep river valleys with its thickets and willow bushes, to the snowy ptarmigan, that dove of icy places. But here in the rocky uplands where I scarcely expected *any* birds to be, the small rock ptarmigan, commonly found among the boulders of the rough Bay coast, increased daily in numbers, and as food for the Indians could readily take the willow ptarmigan's place. Often as we dragged our weird burdens over the lonely snows, we heard the rock ptarmigan's politely questioning chirp. It seemed an appropriate sound indeed: as if amazed, he seemed to be

137

asking, "Who-r-u? Who-r-u? Who-r-u?"

The temperature in the lake country usually dropped at dusk to about 40 degrees below zero. The stars at night were piercingly bright, and it was a nightly temptation, despite weariness, cold and worries, for me to stand outside the tent for a while in the shadows—for after dark there is no safe walking even in the camp—drinking in the hours of mystery that always began with evening. Ekumiak's attitude of awe and fear at this Ungava interior was a primitive response to its powers more impressive than many words.

"Elizaponga" ("I am afraid"), he often said soberly and without shame, as we stood just outside the tent door after supper looking up into the silent heavens.

NOONTIME ON THE TREELINE

At noontimes we found a grove of trees, if possible, trampled out a hard circle in the snow and brushed it with boughs, much as we prepared our tent floors. When near the fire, we were especially careful to knock our clothes free of loose snow, lest it melt and later freeze. (Thus the probable origin of the pretty old Eskimo welcome in which a white visitor was always dusted off with willows.) We always stood on branches near the fire while we lunched.

Doutt and I had notes to make, maps to draw and birds to chase, and the Indians, whenever they were not too tired and we were near thickets, liked to sneak off for some noon ptarmigan hunting. The noon rests were often picturesque scenes. Our well-cased guns, to be kept safe from moisture, were stuck upright in a rough circle in the snow at some distance from us. The three dirty-white rifle-bags of the Indians were decorated insignificantly with thin rings of red and blue braid and with tassels for drawstring trimming, but Daniel's bag was a perfect riot of colours. As we travelled with him, we became more and more interested in the puzzling Daniel Petacumeshcum: a wonderful hunter, vain and jealous of his talents, a subtle precisionist, an enterprising and industrious business man and sometimes, we suspected, a calculating and unscrupulous Indian, if not, indeed, a kind of Ungava Iago! When the trees were scarce or grew so low that they gave us little protection, we sometimes built semicircular wind-breaks by sticking long branches upright into the snow, very close together, and there we all crouched around a few burning sticks.

On those days, crowded close together, we usually simply rested and talked. One grey lonely day, with the world silent and barren all about, Doutt and I crouched near the blaze waiting for the tea water to boil, and discussed the Japanese invasion of China. Our earnest tones and intent faces brought the curious Indians about us in a few moments.

"What are they saying?" the men asked George.

"We are speaking of war," we told George to answer. But George thought for a while and then finally admitted that he knew no word for war in the Indian language.

"Describe it then," we said. "Didn't these Indians ever fight one another?"

"No," said George, "I don't think so."

"Men divide into groups," George told them, translating for us as he went along. "They are enemies. They have guns more terrible than any you can imagine. They shoot off hilltops like this one (pointing) without any trouble. They kill hundreds of men with only one loud shot!" By this time the astonishment and shock of the natives was plain to be seen.

"Do white men shoot each other as we shoot the seal?" asked one of the Ruperts finally, as if he couldn't believe it. When George answered yes, they all looked at each other obviously excited.

Through the afternoon that followed, George told us, the Indians went on discussing this strange thing. It gave a lively air to our party and resulted in loud conversation in the Indians' tent that night. And this was not the only illustration we had of the high regard that the Ungava Indians have for human life. *Nipa* (death)—"the life like a sleep"—they consider a serious thing indeed, and yet their great regard for the state of the soul is in sharp contrast to their indifference toward *suffering*. They may starve or maim each other, but they certainly are unwilling to kill.

One day, for instance, Daniel Petacumeschcum and I cut off from the others to hunt some birds. Our trail led down into a narrow valley. All about us rose slopes in glistening whiteness, broken only by the grey of scattered and windswept boulders and the scrubby green of stunted spruce trees. We flushed a ptarmigan, and as it darted cliffward, Daniel's gun followed its upward flight. But in direct line of fire at that instant appeared the head of one of the men. By a split second, Daniel held his fire. He would have blown that Indian's head off.

Daniel put his face in his hands—even Daniel, *Magetwae*, as the other natives secretly called him, a word meaning the cheater or the man of bad actions— and he wept real tears. When the near-victim joined us, he did not seem astonished at Daniel's passionate embraces. Kissing the lucky fellow on both cheeks, Daniel cried brokenly, *"Sha gat nee pashga sha chee!"* ("I might have shot you!")

Like the escaped hunter, the other Indians accepted the story in typical Indian soberness and silence, but with frightened eyes and long-drawn faces.

Doutt and I used the noon hour for our observations. The sound of a bird note at noon never went unanswered by a visit from me and very few, I think, went unheard even while we were on the trail. Any bird cry was in sharp contrast to our hours of almost painful silence, broken only by the crunch of snowshoes and occasionally by the vibrant low tones of the Indians talking in quick rhythmical fashion to each other as they passed. There is a wide variety of tonal inflection natural to the Indian

140

language when it is spoken by a native, but this beauty is lost when the language is spoken by Old Harold, the Great Whale River interpreter. Old Harold's Indian talk is like a rolling of thunder; he increases in volume as he continues, but his voice stays always on much the same note. The voices of Daniel and Luk Cashe and Jacob Rupert rise and fall musically like a wild river rapids.

Even the Indians would pause to listen to the song of the red-poll, sometimes seizing the occasion to rest for a moment, silently listening with half-smiles on their faces, like figures frozen in the snow. The red-poll has a trill like a wild canary and is the musical sensation of Ungava.

Our white-man's diet was without variation—bannock, jam, stewed dried fruit, oatmeal, bacon, beans and tea. The Indians ate bannock and ptarmigan and drank gallons and gallons of tea. I never knew them to throw away anything. They saved even the used tea leaves, both ours and theirs. Before repacking, we would empty our noontime tea-pails out onto the snow and were disconcerted to see the Indians hunt and scrape afterward to retrieve the frozen clumps of our old tea leaves. And every morning as we broke camp we saw them searching through our brushy floor, upturning the spruce boughs with their poking sticks and picking up every bit of spilled food—bacon, pieces of bannock, even the little tan navy beans that had fallen through the branches from our plates at supper. We were ourselves extremely cautious about waste, and yet the Indians' zeal made us feel almost prodigal. The Indians' rations should have been more than adequate, yet they acted like men on the verge of starvation. We explained it to ourselves by remembering the care that a life of scarcity had taught them to exert.

Luk Cashe at noon was usually the butt of everybody's wit. He could not manage his hot tea-pail, hooking it neatly with a sapling from among the other pails on the fire.

Half the time Luk would drop it, and in trying to rescue the hot thing he would burn his hands. Then young Boyshish and all the others would start laughing, and even Luk, ordinarily good-natured, would laugh if he had nothing but a burn or two. But the simple Luk had his dangerous moments.

Being clumsy as well as simple, Luk Cashe was a veritable menace with a gun. One noontime he hit a ptarmigan without killing it. Our fire was already burning, but we had not yet laid down the boughs to stand on. Frantic with pain the ptarmigan began flopping, moving in a wide circle, swiftly zigzagging as any wounded bird will do to escape capture, dodging wildly in and out among the snowdrifts. Luk aimed at it again and missed it, and aimed and missed it again, and again. Luk had been chopping the firewood a few moments before, and the little hand-axe still stuck where he had left it in the trunk of a tree. With a futile yell of anger Luk finally grabbed up the hatchet, and like the aboriginal savage that he is supposed to have sprung from, he tried to kill the bird with his tomahawk.

He drove the ptarmigan toward us, plainly exulting in his own frenzy, while the wounded ptarmigan, incredibly agile, dragged its snowy wing in convolutions of terror, driven first inward by the dancing Indian, then driven outward by the crackling flames. I would have shot the bird myself but for the insult to Luk the Poor Hunter. And so with the other hushed and gaping onlookers, I watched the pageant unfolding. With the short hatchet raised above his head, his gigantic lanky body and grotesque length of leg bent fantastic for the kill, it was as savage a scene as I ever witnessed.

Some of the Indians had at first been laughing at Cashe for his bad shooting, and Luk was almost crazy-mad. When he finally struck the ptarmigan, it was with such force that the white bird seemed simply to explode upon the snow. The bright blood splattered, the white feathers flew into a bubble and then the maimed body, with

142

crimson head dangling, began to bounce with agony in little silent bounces, scarcely clearing the ground. Luk grabbed for it once, and only got the tail feathers. At the next grab he had the bird. He tore the twitching body apart with his hands and held it up, dripping, in two pieces. His white parka was splashed with crimson. No-one was laughing.

A skillet had been heating on the fire, and Luk almost instantly threw the carcass into the pan. It barely hissed before Luk was gorging himself, his face smeared with blood from the very rare meat. Wolfing down the whole thing himself, Luk presently heaved a great sigh of satisfaction and I saw him afterward with a handful of the feathers wiping blood and grease from his face and hands.

As a matter of fact, all the Indians, even Boyshish, ate ferociously, tearing their thick pan-bread into big pieces and swallowing everything, it seemed, without any chewing. Each carried his own rusty tea-pail, but they all often drank noon tea from a common bucket, unmindful of slurps and other loud noises. They ate openly before us and each other "like dogs and white men," Ekumiak told George once scornfully—forgetting his own manners for a moment. They drank tea clear, never using milk or sugar even though it was offered. They would eat jam whenever they had it, but only with their fingers. They never used forks or spoons, and although they all carried cutting knives in their pockets they never did any spreading. Usually they gulped the juices and gnawed or tore off the meat from the bones of boiled ptarmigan, and fried, as a rule, nothing but bread. Treeline Indians generally boil all fish, birds and animals, and drink up all the cooking-water. All entrails, separately dried, are eaten. Sometimes our helpers cooked their birds without plucking. I have seen their soup with the white feathers floating thickly in it.

We had made no arrangements for Eskimos. Poor

Ekumiak had to eat what we gave him. Our food produced in him no visible emotions as a rule. He seemed to eat without tasting, and kept at noon always in the vicinity of the *kingmee*, George, Doutt or me, mutely asking protection.

The dog was a constant care, but Ekumiak's affection was endless. Tied to the toboggan, the old dog every noon downed a gulp or two of *koweranlu* and *oksu* (rolled oats and seal grease), and then sank into a soft curl, oblivious to everything—the love of Ekumiak, the hostility of Indians, the mystery of seals, the painful paths of science, oblivious even to the hills ahead. Tucking his tender nose under his tail, he would fall at once into a weary noontime nap upon the snow.

The only way we could have beans on the trail at lunch was to cook them up the night before. One evening as George made up the first batch, Doutt looked gravely into the kettle and said, "If you put in two or three teaspoons of soda, they say it takes the 'cackle' out of them."

"That would surely be too much," George told him. I was ignorant of such refinements. But George, being open-minded and in a subordinate position, thought it would do to try the experiment. Thus the beans were boiled up, and that smell was wonderful. It was so wonderful that we all grew optimistic. The weather would be right tomorrow. We knew it! Our socks would all dry by morning. The trail would be easy.

But in the morning the snow was soft. We had a hard time on the trail and long before noon we began to think about beans. At lunch time, while the beans heated up, Doutt and I did our noon exploring, as usual in different directions. I got back to camp as George was making tea.

"Would you like your plate now?" George asked, all too helpfully.

"I sure would," I said—"but where are the beans?" (It was a sort of dark mush that he handed me, with only indications of a bean here and there.) Even the first taste was too much! I spat it out. The stuff was bitter as gall.

144

Seeing George's grin, I looked around for someone else to pass the joke on to. "Here's your plate," I said to Ekumiak.

The big bite he gulped down took him quite by surprise. His cheeks puffed out and he fairly exploded. He jabbered wildly in unknown Husky terms, but seeing us laugh at him he entered into it with us. Pointing off in Doutt's direction and then back to the plate again, Ekumiak suggested that we should also try it on the last of the white men. How he beamed as George presented Doutt with the brimming plate! No-one made a sound, but Ekumiak's eyes were eagerly shining.

"Um! I'm hungry!" cried Doutt, more than ready to feast. He spewed out the whole mouthful, while Ekumiak's chunky shoulders shook, George openly chuckled and I laughed aloud.

The whole batch of beans was useless for eating and there was only time left for hard biscuits and the tea. Ekumiak emptied the bean pot in front of his *kingmee*. The ever-hungry dog awoke and lapped up the mess without a shiver, but for the rest of the day was drag-tailed and trembling, stopping frequently to belch and shake a doleful head. We were somewhat alarmed when even the dog couldn't take it, for we would have sworn before that, that the old Husky could eat anything! We all decided that henceforth the beans should stay natural.

Three days later we sat around after supper, having eaten all the beans we could possibly eat—good strong beans without a drop of soda in them. We were quietly writing notes when the beans began to take effect. The first shot was ignored. (At least it went without comment.) The second brought forth startled smiles from all of us. For a while there was silence. The third 'cackle,' completing our white man's circle, bent the cautious Ekumiak double as he sat on his bed-roll in his accustomed corner. He gurgled, he choked, but was still fighting gamely to be polite. And while trying so hard to keep from laughing, he surprised himself suddenly with his own loud report.

145

It was too much for all of us. We wrecked ourselves, laughing. We pounded the bed rolls and messed up our note-papers. We grew weak, and still laughed. . . .

UNGAVA INTERIOR

Beyond the divide, we were within what by a consensus of opinion we considered to be the Ungava interior. It must be kept in mind as you read this story that we did not come to the Seal Lakes from Great Whale River, but started inland from Richmond Gulf and angled down from the north, and it must also be remembered that in aiming for *Lower* Seal Lake (which lies *north* of the *Upper*), we aimed for the Lake that was nearer to us.

On March 6 near the tenth lake portage, our Indians stopped to hunt and killed twenty rock ptarmigan. Yet as always they were still hungry when we broke camp the next morning. They looked tired, and I felt sure were even more thin that at Richmond Gulf. It was a hard life, but Daniel Petacumeshcum seemed to thrive on it. He too worked hard, but continued to have great nervous energy. He had entire charge of the natives' food and no commissary ever seemed more enterprising. He was a fine hunter, second only in my opinion to the silent, gentle-mannered Jacob Rupert, but Daniel made no use of Jacob's talents. Indeed, Jacob seemed to be endlessly punished. The heavy loads, the long returns for caches, the gruelling and menial camp tasks were always assigned to Jacob Rupert. Every disagreeable job *that had nothing to do with hunting* fell to him. This, of course, it took Doutt and me a long time to realize, and even then we could do nothing about it. In the Ungava interior we were in no position to cross the all-powerful Daniel Petacumeshcum. And Jacob accepted his lot without a word. Jacob could endure anything, George carefully explained to us, as long as he had plenty of tobacco.

On Burnt Wolf Lake and on Clearwater River, which

we reached just after the highest of the terraced hills were passed, it was "cryin' cold!" It was only fourteen below zero, but the hard, wet wind was awful. The Indians were exhausted even by lunchtime. The birds were all sheltered and there was no use hunting. We made camp on March 7 at 2:30 in the afternoon.

On March 8 we were nearing Clearwater Lake,[12] and just before we reached it, we decided to leave our first permanent cache of food, abandoning sufficient rations to get us on our return journey, back to the Gulf. It was a frantic effort to lighten our over-powering load. Doutt and I left the food with qualms, and felt when we did it that "the law of the North," which was supposed to protect all caches, was a pretty flimsy protection. We hoped that the cache would not be seen by anybody, and we remembered that ptarmigan were plentiful in the thickets surrounding Clearwater Lake; even we of little faith did not expect a robbery by anyone who was not terribly hungry.

We made the cache beside our tent circle, cutting the tops off two trees that stood about three feet apart and driving a third support deeply into the snow. We used the three stakes to support a little platform of boughs, a stage as George called it, eight feet above snow level. On top of the platform we left our supplies: 25 pounds of flour, a slab and a half of canned bacon, a tin of jam, three pounds of butter, five pounds of sugar, two tins of corned beef, one pound of coffee and six pounds of lard—from our own stores; from the Indians' reserve, we left twenty pounds of flour, a pork bag, one bag of rolled oats, five pounds of sugar, four pounds of lard and a pound and a half of tea. The stage would keep the food from the reach of wolves or foxes and would keep it from being buried by a heavy snowfall. Daniel Petacumeshcum cut out a message in dots and triangles, the Indian-Eskimo script, on a blazed portion of each of the uprights, explaining that we were depending on this cache to take us all, later, out to Richmond Gulf.

Clearwater Lake is so big that it took us two and a half days to cross the narrow way of it. It is island-sprinkled, shrub-surrounded, bird-haunted and has, in short, a local environment that produces life in unexpected abundance. It has several places of open water, and just above the first rapids 30 rock ptarmigan quietly rested on shore. A flock of 25 red-polls fed among some alder clumps. And on a willow bush just ten inches above the snow, there sat one willow ptarmigan. Most of the islands were deeply wooded, and impressive as a mecca for winter life. Willow ptarmigan as well as rock ptarmigan lived there in great numbers. George told us that on an ancient camp site, on one of the largest Clearwater Lake islands, an Indian encampment composed of a single large teepee, the home of Jacob Rupert, stood. Clearwater Lake, in our minds, was a landmark. From Clearwater Lake, Daniel had said long ago, we should be led directly into Lower Seal Lake.

For the next three days we continued to walk from *seebe* to *sakgaheegan* (river to little lake), and little lake to river, with tiny falls and rapids between them or perhaps rocky overland stretches. We thought that undoubtedly we neared the Seal Lakes region, but so broken up is the winter landscape between snow, rocks and water, that I can scarcely trust the maps I made of it.

The Indians grew more and more talkative as we moved farther inland, recounting the grim tales that they had heard about the place and often speaking of the 21 Indians who had died there of starvation in 1930. They began to pay homage to the heroic Luk Cashe and to young Boyshish, who had been two of the only three survivors. But poor Luk and poor Boyshish, I am sure, were even more frightened than the others.

Our Indians were far from familiar with the paths we took, but they had an astonishing memory for landmarks. Rocks and turnings that they insisted to George they had seen only once, perhaps, they would recall even before we came to them. We were passing a small spruce grove, indistinguishable to me from any of the others, when Luk Cashe suddenly dropped his tow-line. Stepping out of the circle he swung off silently, while we watched and waited, making a rest-time of it, until Luk reappeared bearing a gun. He had abandoned it the year before when his load was too heavy, and had lodged it safely in a tree. What did it matter to Luk that in order to get it he might have to cross over half a dozen small mountains? Without the toboggans the miles would have meant little to the Indians. Free and half-starved, in the long winter seasons of the old days of the Ungava caribou, the natives ranged throughout the interior every winter, hunting and trapping. But the poor modern hunters who must rely entirely upon guns and ammunition do not dare to range freely or to get very far from known fishing places.

As we neared the Seal Lakes we became increasingly impatient. It was especially hard to resign ourselves to the loss of every Sunday, for Daniel was a minister and he would not travel then. Ekumiak, too, carried a piece torn from a post calendar and kept track of the holy day scrupulously. He, too, was a minister. Daniel said a Sunday service every Sabbath in the Indians' tent, and to our amazement Ekumiak went over one Sunday and sat with them. In my own tent I could hear them singing incomprehensible words to the tune of "Jesus Loves Me."[13]

There was plenty of work to occupy our evenings, and even our Sundays. We wore three pairs of socks apiece, light inner duffle moccasins and moosehide moccasins. Every night, this whole collection had to be hung up to dry. Our footgear did not leak, but the socks and inner moccasins would absorb perspiration and the outer sealskin boots would soak up an astonishing amount of moisture. Our feet always *felt* warm and dry, but all footgear would need drying every night. It was a scramble to see whose things would get up first, for the one dependable drying place was immediately over the stove; as the first things dried, the others would have to be shifted to the good spot. Our drying line of heavy cord was strung just under the ridgepole of the tent, and while our things were drying, Doutt and I wrote our notes up and then George and I usually played rummy. The light from our candles was barely sufficient, and Ekumiak, who had great scorn for *naputa*, the white man's candle, often boasted to George of the Eskimo lamp—the *kudlu* as he lovingly abbreviated the term *kudliak*—which he would make for us from the oil of the five inland seals he would kill. Ekumiak spoke often of this excellent haul that he expected to bring in immediately from the mysterious lake home of *kasagea*. We would read our papers with a *kudlu* tonight, he used to assure George each morning determinedly, after we reached the Seal Lakes region.

Our mitts, especially, were always wringing wet because they were made out of sealskin, which absorbs moisture at a great rate yet strangely retains warmth, and even when wet will not admit water. The sealskin float (used in walrus hunting) always floats, and the sealskin kayak, however clammy, is always waterproof.

Sitting in the tent at night, we wore the dry clothing intended for next day. When we went to the toilet outside, before we slept, we wore our low inside moccasins, but we kept well in the path already stamped down. If we wandered in Ungava where no paths were beaten, we certainly did not choose the time of darkness for it.

I could not keep in paths of course when I hunted birds, and I often hit buried logs with the toes of my snowshoes and pitched headlong into a drift—a six-foot well of snow. There was no climbing out of it with snowshoes on. Placing the shoes on the snow surface carefully, I churned and packed a little hard space around me until finally I could flounder out of the hole and manoeuvre into the snowshoes as they stood at the edge of the hole, ready-placed and waiting.

The Indians slept entirely without blankets (with the single exception of Boyshish), in a kind of traditional huddle formation, much like fancy swimmers "making the rose." Their feet pointed toward the stove in the centre, their heads lying outward toward the tent walls. They seemed to sleep only at intervals. Someone was always awake to stoke the fire, and he no doubt talked to whoever would talk with him. Sometimes they would rise all together and gossip sociably in the middle of night, drinking tea, perhaps, smoking, and then settling down again for another nap. Having no bedding, they doubtless found it necessary to stir often. The snow floor was so close under their spruce boughs that they could at any time stretch down a poking finger and feel the iciness of if. To a fantastic extent, the Indians seemed determined to live as freely as the birds, but unlike the birds they could not simply fluff out their feathers (thus increasing the size of the empty air spaces that provide birds with insulation), to take care of the variations in Ungava temperature.

Young Boyshish, who had been in a position at the post to see what comfort there is in things white men do, used his blanket proudly, hole and all. There were blankets in all the permanent Indian teepees, but when Indians travel they will never be encumbered. Boyshish had learned, moreover, a fact of great importance that he once mentioned to George. He had learned that white men in the North are usually healthier than Indians. Boyshish was a smart lad, and grew up remarkably fast under the strenuous tutelage of the trail. He developed *musquav*, as the Indians said, meaning that in strength, fortitude and judgment, Boyshish became almost a man. In a few cruel weeks (almost *too* quickly, it seemed to me) he left his boyhood behind him. He started out with the lightest load, but, excluding Luk Cashe, he ended up with as great a load as any.

Twice, the Indians' supply of wood ran low during the night. It caused great commotion in their tent, for of course none wanted to go out woodchopping in the drifts in the darkness. We heard the excited wrangling, the angry voices, the clear, light, persuasive tones of young Boyshish. By and by, when it was again silent, we heard the shuffling sound of snowshoed feet, and the ringing, steady blows of the axe. Despite all the talk, Luk Cashe was both times the victim, for Boyshish could easily find arguments sufficient to impress Cashe's sleepy, confused and unsubtle mind. Cashe the mighty, the only man among the Indians who could safely have defied everybody on everything, the only one who could safely have refused *ever* to go, was the only one who ever went.

On the trail next morning, Boyshish the witty would be sure to laugh at the recollection of the night-chopping, reminding Luk of the dismal going-out, of the cold, of the frozen iron-like bark of the trees, of the irritating soft deep snow. Whereupon Luk, although both sullen and angry, would be beset with a conflict of emotions, for although he certainly hated to be laughed at, he loved to be looked at even more. Unable to make up his mind whether or not to be angry, he would swing along the trail, confused and muttering, not noticing where he went, furnishing the rest with fresh laughter as he yanked his load over bumps that could have been avoided or sank to his knees in the edge of a snow drift that he stupidly stepped upon.

What a wild man Luk was! He seemed to start chopping wood at night without judgment or preparation, just to see a tree before him and immediately to lay into it— wham! While others were still thinking that the next move should be some wood, Luk would probably have felled his first tree. Often he would plunge into our midst without thought of consequences, dragging a whole tree, unshaved, under each of his powerful arms. If they hit a bush in the course of transit, it did not record in Luk's mind as a problem. His solutions to all problems was simply to yank. And yank he did, without malice or forethought or any looking back. Whether he uprooted some hitherto immovable bush or scooped up some unwary soul who had not seen him coming, Luk was

152

impervious. *"Yawkwa! Yawkwa!"* ("Look out!") cried the Indians often, and "Look out for Cashe!" was George's warning cry of evenings whenever there was cutting and Luk was on the loose. No-one held catastrophes against good old Luk. An innocent Gulliver, he moved among all the fearful Little People.

Of mornings, everything was hurry-hurry in the camp. Although they had been up and down all night talking, drinking and smoking (especially Jacob Rupert who could not bear many moments even at night without tobacco), the Indians were always through breakfast before we were. And when an Indian is ready to move, he moves! Not so, we.

Our tent life was as restful as we could make it. Every evening before George turned into his sleeping-bag, he would cut up a neat pile of wood-shavings that he stored close to his hand, so that without rising in the morning he could reach out and put the shavings in the stove and even strike the match and hold it lighted to the kindling. No-one in our tent ever stirred until he was forced to. The sounds that George made at the stove and the odour of bacon and coffee (while we still had some) always woke me to a pleasant scene. The tent would be warm. The frying-pan would rattle as George shook it over the fire. There was a heavy roaring from the stove itself. Always at that moment in the day, how vain, stale and unprofitable seemed all well-explored professions.

The birds loved the early morning hours. Wild as they were, unlike the willow ptarmigan of the rivers, the small white rock ptarmigan sometimes fed very near us when I first stepped from the tent in the morning. They were so hungry, after their long night of fasting, that at this hour their shyness would be less than their hunger.

George usually fed us oatmeal and bacon for breakfast, with tea or coffee, and he always had a hectic time trying to wash up the dishes before the Indian horde descended to take down the tent. Generally, he was in the midst of the job when they all swarmed in. It was an avalanche of

153

movement that every morning demolished our little shelter. The stove would still be burning brightly, but an Indian would grab the smokepipe between two little logs of wood, pinching it securely, and would rip it out piece by piece, dropping the pieces into the drifts to cool. While our tent rolled in a blue haze of smoke and our eyes and nostrils burned with it, two heavy sticks would be inserted beneath the stove. As deftly as I would lift a pancake on a turner, the Indian would lift up the light tin contraption that still belched flames from its open pipe hole, menacing our canvas. Then cautiously, with all hands backed away and everyone watching, the dark-faced hunter would teeter to the door. That moment was always tense, and the next one triumphant, as the stove was thrown into the snow.

Camp-breaking, in my memory, is always exactly the same. There in the drift, the stove spits, hisses and whoofs, billowing in steams, while the handler crouches over it catching his breath and letting the tin cool a trifle before he inserts a stick into the chimney hole and tips the stove over. Then as he gingerly shakes it, the door to the bottom, the ashes flow on the wind. The unburned sticks tumble out flaming redly, lie on the whiteness for a fading moment, and the last puffs of blue smoke rise into the air. All is still. All is done. The charred chunks sink in silence into the snow. Ekumiak through it all stands motionless and soundless. He can never accept this thing without showing the old fear in his eyes. It is a dreadful symbol of the might of the Indians, this swift doing away with *keachaute*—the hot stove.

With the stove out of the way, the Indians attack the tent, grabbing up everything without discrimination. We had learned early that the best thing was to flee. George is half-wild. The slops seep into the floor where he has suddenly dashed them. He ducks his head and hopes nothing will hit him as he dries the dishpan and tries to stow it away. Heavy feet are kicking out the guy-ropes.

Heavy hands are grabbing up boughs from the floor. The tent roof bounces and bangs as the Indians begin to whack the canvas sharply to break off the profusion of icicles, which go rolling and rattling down. The tent must be clean and dry before it is repacked upon a toboggan. (Luk Cashe was never allowed to beat the tent roof, because some judgment had to be exercised when the bough was chosen.)

The scrambling Indians doubtless work to some set pattern, but they always seem to be everywhere at once. Untied from the ridgepole, the pairs of shears are pushed over and fall silently into the snow. The canvas comes off the ridgepole with the two sides already folded together. The ridge tapes are untied, and the tent makes a final small rectangle and is slipped into the tent bag. Camp-breaking is over. Gone is the warmth, the deep sleep, the smoke, the flames, the swinging socks and the note-papers. We are once again at the mercy of the trail. . . .

The Indians hang around the camp site, turning back those floor boughs still remaining in the circle, greedily searching underneath them for scraps of our food. George is packing up the round, fibre food cases where the pots and pans are nested, along with our knives, forks and perishables in their moisture-proof paraffin sacks. Ekumiak and the old dog stand hitched to their sled leashes, waiting.

As we neared the Seal Lakes region, the spring light suddenly brightened into a torturing glare. We white men all put on snowglasses, trusting the natives to do whatever was necessary. The natives did nothing. In two days, their unprotected eyes were all bloodshot, and on the third morning, two of them went entirely blind, and had to be led! When George questioned them, half in passion, they explained it shruggingly: *"Sesh-tee-shik."* ("It is only snow-blindness.")

The three hard days after we left Clearwater Island were full of strain for us, the strain of impatient expectancy and the dreadful dazzle of the sun. I forced myself to think calmly about the summer, and if possible not to think of the Belchers at all. I would be a true man of the North, I said. I would be cheerful at all costs. I would be a real fatalist. But still I was a man of two lives, one an Ungava plodder stolidly thumping through the snows, the other a waiter and a watcher of the ice bridge to Tukarak.

The rock boulders of the Seal Lakes region were of tremendous size. On 11 March, with the sun warm and the air pleasant (the temperature was five degrees above zero), we suddenly emerged from behind a boulder onto a thin strip of spreading ice. No bands played. No flags flew. But the ice-hung rims of shore, the distant hills gently rolling, with reindeer-lichen palely greening the wide plains of climax-tundra, the triumphant cries of the seeing Indians and the straining faces of the two who were blind, told us even before Daniel's pointing and George's shout that this was the memorable moment.

"Look!" cried George. "It's the southern arm of Lower Seal Lake!" In long white frozen curves of ice and thickets, the mysterious waters that caverned *kasagea* lay finally before us.

"Tana!" ("That's it!") breathed Ekumiak, awestruck, as the truth at last dawned on him also.

Like Clearwater Lake, this inland water was a shrub-surrounded haven for birds. Fifteen flocks of ptarmigan flew over us on the first two miles of the march, coming to rest always on the rocky shore-points where the Arctic willows thickly grew, supplying food. As we turned northward following the bends of the Arm toward the main Seal Lake, we saw off to the west of us a distant knotty range of hills. There, I thought, must be the source of the famous, long, swift Nastapoka River.

The southern arm of Lower Seal Lake was thick with islands heavily wooded on shores and slopes, but we had yet to see the main circle of the water. We trudged on

until four in the afternoon and made our night camp
then, with the arm waters beginning to widen where the
arm and lake proper were beginning to meet.

Caribou (there was no doubt about it) had lately visited
the spot. They had been pawing up lichens on the tops of
the two islands, which in my excitement I immediately
visited. Hudsonian chickadees and Canada jays were
plentiful. A flock of red-polls set up a loud crying beyond
a ridge as soon as I came near them. A good omen for
seals, I thought, my spirits soaring, that there should be
so many birds. We were still several hour's march from
the open water that we should hunt in, but to my mind,
today was the day!

For the next six days, six long bitter eerie incredible days,
we hunted for the seal on Lower Seal Lake, without
success. The men grew daily hungrier, more sullen and
more openly afraid. They were full of superstitions.
Achic-o-sakgaheegan, we discovered, had always been a
name to conjure with. Even before we reached the Lakes,
Daniel had paused one day by a rock with a running
stream of water over it. He had lifted his face fearfully
toward the rock, laying his hand on George's arm and
asking him to listen.

"Can't you hear the Little Brown Dog barking?" he had
whispered, describing the ghostly spirit of a long-dead
animal whose voice like a barking dog could always be
heard through the falling water. "The old people talk
about it," said Daniel. "Whenever they pass this place in
the summer, they begin to hear the Little Brown Dog
running to meet them. Can't you hear it barking?"

This remark caused us some uneasiness, and for two
reasons. Not only did we dread to see in operation this
unknown power of beliefs and traditions so difficult for
us to understand and to cope with, but we now understood that Daniel had been lying when he had protested
that he did not know the interior. We were not wholly
amazed when he pointed off to the left one day with a

wild exclamation and cried to George, "See that island there? On that very island my own son was born!"

Clearly, Daniel, although he was a fine hunter and an efficient foreman, was not to be trusted. He continued to be extremely useful to us, for he was not only remarkably able on the trail but also in the seal hunt, yet he was so fiercely jealous of Jacob Rupert (the only native who understood how to use our ancient seal nets) that he was almost beside himself. I hate to think of what might have happened if Jacob's net had at once been able to ensnare *kasagea*—but it is a stupid supposition. Persistently, hopefully, keeping the old chin up all the time, we hunted at the first hole on Lower Seal Lake for six days, finding it impossible to accept the naked evidence that we hunted in vain.

Four of the natives became totally blind all at one time and were confined to the tent. Only Jacob Rupert and Daniel still had good eyes, and only Jacob, it seemed, knew how to make "glasses." (*"Sesh-tee-shi-kapse,"* Jacob called them.) Seeing the fine wooden ones he had made for himself, we bribed him with tobacco to make them for everybody—even those who seemed already past help. But we might well have spared him the trouble. Indians, the blind men told us, did not *like* to wear glasses. Even Boyshish, usually rational, wore his but half a day before he declared flatly that he would wear them no more. His eyes were bright pink and running pro-fusely; they stung, he said, as if sand had been rubbed into them, yet he clung like the others to the native belief that if he endured his first attack for four or five days more he would be immune to snow-blindness for the rest of the spring! We were mute with disgust, but we trusted that in the dark of the tent they would somewhat recover.

At last we accepted the fact that the first open water of Lower Seal Lake was going to yield us nothing. Neither Daniel, nor Jacob, nor the Eskimo Ekumiak with his old sniffing *kingmee*, nor Doutt, nor I, out from sunrise to sunset, could find any traces of *kasagea*.

What was there to do but to move on? There was no reason to break this camp and to build ourselves another, except for the feeling of moving; one more day spent in the same location in which we had just finished the first fruitless six would have been almost unbearable.

If not in the southern waters, then perhaps the seals might be wintering in the uncharted river region just north of Lower Seal Lake. It was Daniel's idea, I suspect. And so into this region, still with hope, our Indians blindly dragging their toboggans like a gang of prisoners, we moved the whole camp on 17 March. "Twenty days," we remembered the Indians at Richmond Gulf to have said, and how we had scoffed at the suggestion of giving all that time simply to the trail. But already it had been twenty days.

It would not be our fault, we decided, if at *this* camp we did not find *kasagea*. We adopted procedures of fantastic caution. We never moved except singly, stepping glidingly, avoiding any "thump." No guns were fired—which meant doing without ptarmigan.

Jacob Rupert was just setting the seal net over a swift current of open water when Doutt declared that he saw a seal! I too had seen it, but I thought that what I saw was an animal's back, which a seal never shows. Yet such differences of opinion really were of no matter. The important fact was that we had both seen something! With complete precaution we once more moved our camp to rid the vicinity of all possible sounds of confusion. Three or four miles ahead we pitched the two tents again, and our stumbling hunters, as excited as we at the possibility of seal meat, even put on their glasses.

But Daniel Petacumeshcum, at this first real news about *kasagea*, seemed stung as by gadflies. Jacob Rupert was ordered back from the net to oversee camp building, while Daniel with face set and voice tense said to George, "Stay back!" He explained to George that he knew of more open water even farther beyond, and that he would go there but he must go alone, and he struck out with only his gun.

It was noon when he left us. At 4:30, with daylight almost faded, he came running into camp, shaking, dishevelled and terribly excited. He too had seen a seal! And he had shot it! But he had lost it afterward—it was under the ice now, dead, floating somewhere in the water. He was almost weeping with chagrin and cold.

Knowing his motives, we did not more than half-believe him, but winter had already come back, and the wet and bitter day had made the long hours of creeping over the lake ice on hands and knees, and possibly lying flat on the stomach, a terrible ordeal. Perhaps Daniel really had shot a seal. But it was too dark now to hunt for it any more.

The next day we moved our camp again. Living halfway between the two main stretches of open waters, we began to chop holes in the ice where Daniel had done his "killing" as he insistently described it, and there we lay stretched flat on the ice, congealed with cold, hour after hour, looking for the carcass of a dead *kasagea*. We studied the paths of the swift-moving currents, drilling roads of peep-holes along what seemed to be the course of the currents. Cleared ice-patches admitted much light. We accustomed our eyes to the under-ice world, seeing another life operating there in the freedom of the winter stream. We watched the bubbles, the mossy fronds of the rock bottom, the swirls of the rapids, the floating occasional sluggish winter fish, with our weary heads supported on our mitts, until we were dizzy, but we saw no signs of a brown heavy object with the shining hide of a dead *kasagea*.

We pushed the hunt forward in every possible way. Each one had his turns watching at the net, lest the net should take a seal that might fight away afterward. The net was suspended across the current and so rigged that if a seal struck it, his weight would draw the bag securely around him. Not being able to rise to the surface to

160

breathe (as seals must do about every twenty minutes), he would be drowned. That at least was the theory. It would have been wonderful to have had such a specimen, without a wound, intact and whole.

The cold wind and wetness and the lack of meat for the Indians made more deadly than ever this time of crisis. But in spite of everything, Ekumiak's aggressive will seemed scarcely less than Daniel's. He left our tent every morning at dawn accompanied by the *kingmee,* that sober, soundless, faithful old dog! As his people have always done, the little Eskimo went alone, but no longer confident of any but one fact—that at least in *suffering* he could outdo them all. Hour after hour he trudged the shores and sent the *kingmee* sniffing the broad ice, baffled and indignant at such unnatural creatures as seals that apparently had no holes!

The old dog at last did smell out a few holes, but no matter how patiently we each crouched and waited scarcely breathing, no-one was ever called upon to lift the harpoon. Ekumiak built snowblock shelters for us to wait in, little curved "hides" like roofless igloos to protect us from the wind. Day after day, in frozen silence, we waited at our holes. Certainly it was not from a want of trying, of planning or believing (or praying, as Ekumiak told George he did every night), that we camped at the second inland hunting water for six more days without getting a seal!

We went through a period of blackness then, which I thought at the time would be our worst. Already for twelve days we had hunted the mysterious *kasagea*—with no success. I came in at noon, or near it. We had tea. I had been out since the first hour of daybreak, sitting and waiting, staring at the hole of open water with my eyes never leaving it, my mind never relaxing, until I could stand it no longer. There was such a thing, I thought, as doing too much! There was such a thing as wearing out stupidly, to no end. There was such a thing as being predestined to failure. I really *was* down.

I entered the tent and looked about me. There was an air of unreality about the place. Ordinarily I considered it a fine thing to be living in a tent but on this particular day the piny odour of the spruce boughs from our newly brushed floor almost sickened me with the travesty that this place was a real home.

It was too much like home not to be painful. Here I slept warmly in my eiderdown bag, almost as comfortably as in a bed. Here in the evening I played a little rummy with the soft-voiced George, and wrote my notes up, cheerfully remembering the long day and enjoying evening. But of late there had been no peace, no rummy, no warmth in my life—nothing but dread and discouragement.

I sat down wearily with nostalgic memories, flipping over the pages of the camp book that had been with me for so many years. I read through the remedy for snake bites, the description of diseases, the directions on how to pitch a tent (very amusing), advice on how to approach a bear, and a recipe for apple pie. . . .

The recipe for apple pie did something to me. I had a sudden fierce yearning for domesticity—for a warm place, with things being stirred up in a bowl! And suddenly I had the will to do.

"How'd you fellows like an apple pie for dinner?" I asked, creating a silence so shocked that you might think we had just heard a baby crying. I had kept my voice casual, as if apple pie for dinner were just something I hadn't got around to before. There was a cynical look on Doutt's face when I glanced at him, and a wondering look on George's, and in Ekumiak's eyes was an eager willingness to be perfectly agreeable no matter what I was proposing.

"Who's gonna provide it?" asked Doutt tauntingly, while George's mouth began to twitch in an effort not to smile too much.

"I just found a recipe," I answered calmly. "I'm thinking of trying it!" With a steady voice I read the recipe aloud to see whether or not we had all the ingredients: flour, lard, salt, apples, sugar. We had. George obligingly set out the sack of dried apples and began to fix a little more fire.

At first I was self-conscious. Whenever I looked at the others there was a glance of mutual suspicion between us and a kind of secret gleeful smirk replaced their ordinarily kind expressions. But I produced my own idea of an air of efficiency and nonchalance. "Steady," I told myself. "Keep a cheerful countenance. Don't act bothered. Don't hurry. Be cool. Read carefully, and think about this as if it were an experiment in the laboratory. Take your time. *Enjoy* yourself!"

I am not a remarkable man. My pancakes do not make a figure eight in the air as I lightly flip them over with an agile turner, but I have stirred up "camp muck" ever since I can remember. My discrimination in the matter of food is only a little beyond Ekumiak's, and yet I very much like to eat. Mrs. Houghton used to bake apple pie for me nearly every day when I was in the University. "Mr. Twomey *likes* it so much," she would explain apologetically to the others when they suggested less pie and more ice cream. Mrs. Houghton had great sympathy with me because I spent so much time "with the birds," and she had a real comprehension of the influence that pie exerts upon a graduate student.

With laboratory precision, I got out the necessary tools. The piepan would have to be one of our tin eating plates. For measuring ("You're just a dub! Good cooks don't measure!"), we had tin cups and teaspoons. From the large paraffin bag I took out three cups of dried apples and put them in a pail of water to soak up and to cook a little on top of the stove. While they simmered cozily, with soft watery sounds, I dumped flour onto a cloth laid on top of a packing-case. By this time I was dusty white in my stomach regions, but I had begun to enjoy myself long before.

It was an age-old urge that I was following. There was a

163

real kick to it. I am sure that I moved neatly and performed all the little operations of rolling out the dough and such things with dispatch and even with some grace. The flour dropped upon the floor made no mess, for it sifted through the green spruce boughs easily and soon disappeared. With my knife, and occasionally with my fingers, I mixed the lard and flour together. There were, it is true, places where lard seemed to be the chief ingredient, yet on the whole it gained the semblance of dough that might soon become a piecrust. I believe that the recipe had suggested baking powder, which both George and I, after our experiment with beans, knew to be not good for the stomach. My piecrust was made without it.

"What do you call this?" queried Doutt, as I energetically rubbed my hands above the kneading board trying to free my fingers from sticky lumps of goo.

"I'm not naming it until it's done," I answered in the accepted words and manner. "Good cooks *never* do that."

This ancient wheeze was full of dewy freshness for George. He slapped his thigh impulsively at my comeback and let out one of his rare, short, almost bird-like chuckles. I had mixed up the dough in one of our round pails and rolled it out with a medicine bottle. It was plain that George respected my ingenuity. He was instinctively my friend, moreover, for did we not play rummy together on those long evenings that could have been so lonely?

Ekumiak had gone out again long ago. He had decided to take another turn at watching by the holes. No doubt the cheerfulness and activity had inspired him. He would wait, he told George, smilingly. Before the pie was finished, we had all been, as it were, renewed.

I did experience one dreadful moment when I realized that we had no oven. Of course we didn't! Why had I ever thought we did? The pie was ready. It looked like a real pie. I had punched generous holes all over it to let the steam escape. I had left the indentations of my thumb all around the edges. I had wanted to use up all the apples,

164

and the center of the pie rose in a luscious-looking hump. There would be fat, whole-hearted pieces when it was done, something into which to sink the old tushes! But without an oven, would it ever *be* a pie? I admit I had my doubts. But if it must cook on top of the stove, then it must. And it did.

I put a lid over the pie to begin with, let it cook for some time that way, got scared and removed the lid for the second half of the operations. The thing cooked for a long while. The afternoon wore on with smells enough in the tent to drive us all crazy. The juice, melted with butter and sugar, ran down from the steam holes as the pie bubbled and burped chummily and syrupy drippings fell and burned upon the stove top with incredibly promising fragrance. The sneerers had not been sneering for some time. The tent got warmer and warmer, and the smells richer and richer. The place was for a moment "an opium dream of forgetfulness." The seal, the snows, the terrible wind, the tired muscles and the wet clothes—all slipped away and peace stole in.

They all took a proprietary interest, giving the pie close and motherly scrutiny from time to time as if *they* had made it. I said nothing, but I felt indignant. About four o'clock it gave signs of shrivelling up. We waited for it to brown, but it didn't. It had a creamy cooked look, however, and was, we all agreed, undoubtedly done! We lifted it from the stove to cool. George began to get more supper ready. Little Ekumiak came back looking frozen but cheerful. Doutt and I went out together for a while, checking at the net and consulting with the various watchers of the earlier afternoon. No luck!—as we knew. But our minds were not dark when we returned to the tent a little after five. There would be pie. . . .

How we admired ourselves as we sat down to a warm meal, the pie standing on top of the packing-case between the two candles like an idolatrous object of temple worship. We ate it all. It was soggy and thick, "like a cobbler," Doutt said critically.

"I call it a pie," I answered, and George beamed at the little joke and at the dripping piece that he held in his hand. They ate with gusto and no more comment. "How is it?" I finally asked, mortally ashamed to be asking and offended that they had not volunteered the kind word.

"Not bad," said Doutt, while George grinned pleasantly and took another enormous bite.

Was that all? I wondered, my heart sinking. Just to sit there, callously eating away the fruits of my rapture, and say just "not bad!" And suddenly there came to me a vision of the hurt eyes of Mrs. Houghton, long ago. Suffer and learn.

"How it is, Mr. Twomey?" she used to ask when she brought the second serving, no doubt ashamed to ask as I was now, and week after week expecting, against all experience to the contrary, that I would say something more than, "Not bad!"

Ekumiak finished his allotment with his usual disinterested and rapid chewing. I could well imagine what *he* thought: was this something special or not? If so, why? If not, why all the talking? They call it a *pie*—a strange word for a strange taste. But no matter. It was food. One chewed a moment. One thought carefully of nothing. Then all went quickly down into the stomach.

DRAMA AT SEAL LAKES

Doutt during these trying days hardly said a word. On 21 March, from nine in the morning until five at night, we and the Indians and Ekumiak covered every hole that we knew of, for every minute of the time, without finding any sign of a seal. During all these hours everyone was perfectly quiet, sitting in the separate "hides" of snow that Ekumiak had built for us.

While I sat in my own "hide," I heard a pair of jays fussing in a clump of trees behind me. The sun was out again but it was stinging cold. A red-poll flew over, giving

166

his clear ringing song as he passed into the distant hills. A single Hudsonian chickadee winged above our strange community—as it must have seemed to him—stopping for a moment's rest on a large rock boulder that stuck up from the ice only a few feet from me, and was off again with an excited chirp. Two flocks of rock ptarmigan whizzed by like bullets, flying but a few scant feet above the ground. I sat almost motionless through the whole day, until the fading light and bitter evening chill drove us all at last in a common misery back to camp. George and Jacob Rupert had got in from their far searches before me and with the same old story: "no *kasagea*."

That night we did not hear Jacob's rich tenor voice singing "In the Land of the Sweet By and By." The Indians' food condition was precarious, and only our own woes and the intentness of our search for the seal had kept us from inquiring much into it. We did not dare to let them shoot within sound of the shrub-bordered lake or river for fear of alarming *kasagea*, and beyond the shrubs there were no birds. According to our calculations, there should still have been reserves of food from the toboggans, but Daniel said he had given out the last they had. We were too absorbed in our schemes to ask why. We simply split our own remaining rations, giving half to the Indians, and prepared to quit. Twenty-five pounds of flour, fifteen pounds of beans, ten pounds of split peas and a little bacon would keep them alive until we could all reach the cache of abandoned supplies just beyond Clearwater Lake Island. My heart was like lead that night and I could hardly look at Doutt, knowing what he must feel. The Indians had been on the point of mutiny long before this, and we knew now that they could not be kept inland any longer. Later on that day we meant to let the Indians shoot, but the wind was up and all the birds were under cover.

For the *kingmee* Ekumiak was still in tortures of fear, but he himself was no longer afraid of the Indians. At least he was no longer afraid of young Boyshish. Boyshish knew a little Husky, so that the two of them could have a glimmering of conversation together, and sometimes Ekumiak had gone so far as to sit in the Indians' tent singing hymns with them, for they knew the same tunes, though in different language. On the night of March 21, he furnished them with a drama, a pantomimed story from traditional Eskimo life.

The Indians lounged around the tent walls in various postures, looking positively gaunt. They were all muttering among themselves when I came in and they continued to mutter. George was there, having come like me in restless aimlessness. I sat down at George's invitation, and against our general policy, being too tired and careless now to take heed of dignity or of lice any longer. The red-stove glowed and crackled. The row of swinging mitts, fantastically dangling from the drying-rack near the ceiling, grew enormous in my eyes, hanging there as a horrible symbol of our sufferings and our defeat. Twelve tired, wet, frozen, *empty* hands. Empty stomachs. Tired, baneful, bloodshot eyes, I thought, watching them. What could we do except quit?

Were the Indians talking of risking it just one more day, George asked Daniel, but Daniel had already told Doutt that they wouldn't. They hadn't wanted to risk it for the last week or more. And who could blame them? As to the food stores, weird suspicions were always crossing our minds, dark and unprovable. The fact remained that there were not even rations enough to make the home-going easy, and the men were in no shape to bear much more suffering. *"Undyeskosen"* (I am tired"), *"Undowksin"* ("I am sick"), *"Kewaida!"* ("Let's go home!") they were muttering on all sides.

Their voices rose in malevolence as Daniel's rose in argument. There was a pause presently, with things apparently hopeless. All sat dejected and most of them silent. *"Sheewadan"* ("I am hungry"), added Luk Cashe simply, summing it all up in a nutshell.

But Ekumiak and Boyshish, who had been speaking

168

together, suddenly held up their hands, motioning to the Indians to move back out of the way, and Boyshish began explaining to the group excitedly that Ekumiak was going to show them all the *pibors dowhoon*—the winter hunt of the Inuit.

"He will show them," whispered George for my benefit, "how the Eskimos used to hunt seals long ago."

The Indians were looking up with an amazing show of interest—for *them*—as Ekumiak, holding out his hand to me, asked, *"sernuhuti?"*—for the watch out of my pocket. He put the watch on the food-box near him, first holding it up to show the dial and pointing to four o'clock. His body sagged, his eyes closed, his face dropped. He stretched himself on the floor and slept.

"Tabiscow" ("darkness"), murmured Boyshish in hushed tones as the actor indicated that it was night.

Ekumiak's pantomime was very realistic. He sat up, yawned, shivered. He stood up, turned to the stove to warm his hands a moment, then dug out a hole from the real *apputi* with his real *puteru* (jack-knife), as if he were in his igloo, and pretended to urinate into it. (George and I laughed aloud, and Ekumiak glanced at us with a waggish expression of the actor's gratitude. But all the while he was in dead earnest.) He pulled on a pair of pants, and then pulled on another, holding up two fingers so that we understood.

"Two pairs," whispered George to me helpfully as Boyshish explained again to the Indians. Then Ekumiak donned a parka and repeated the operation also. Two parkas! He put on several pairs of socks and pulled on high boots (tightening the drawstring high at the top so that we understood he meant the Eskimo *komik*). He put on two pairs of mitts. He pulled up one parka hood. Then he pulled up the other. Again he went to the stove. Again he shivered. Then he gave a great sigh of resignation. After that he acted swiftly, gathering up objects, first a *long* one as he measured it for us by his arms. ("The harpoon," whispered George, entranced.) Then he hastily revolved one hand about the other in cylindrical fashion, as if winding the long harpoon line about his arm. Down on his hands and knees, he moved forward in a determined crawl, out through the long low tunnelled entrance of the imaginary igloo. Turning to us with a smile, which served very well for the first act curtain, he rose and showed us the watch again, pointing to only a little past four.

There was nothing startling in what Ekumiak did at any time, but somehow we felt that there was. The little Inuk had that subtle inborn quality of being able to command attention. Like many fine actors he was not much when he was himself, but given licence to be somebody else, his strength was tremendous. Once he had decided to entertain us, he threw his whole soul into it, and was rewarded with a complete success. No Broadway prize play was ever more hung upon by a gaping audience than was Ekumiak's little drama in that drab tent in the Ungava wilderness.

For almost half an hour in reality (and for many hours as revealed upon the watch), we sat in spirit beside an Eskimo's seal hole, with tension in the tent rising to an ever higher pitch. Even the Indians lost themselves in Ekumiak's acted story. Shifting his feet with incredible care among the spruce boughs on the tent floor, the Eskimo would indicate strained muscles—so tired that they must be moved, but moved without the slightest sound. Intermittently, he would show us the watch dial, solemnly and painfully moving his finger completely around the face of it, indicating that the seal hunter in the drama had waited one hour, then that he had waited two, then three, four, five, six, seven and eight.

At the end of ten imaginary hours, Ekumiak picked up the fingers of one hand and let the hand fall limply, as if it were frozen. Then the little Inuk scooped up some snow, very cautiously, very silently, as always, and began rubbing the limp hand back and forth, slowly, over and over. A gasp went up from the watching Indians at the look of suffering on the fat Eskimo face of Ekumiak, as he sat clasping the supposedly frozen fingers tightly between his legs.

Five more hours went by, as he made plain on the clock. Ekumiak's body was drawn into a knot of misery. His eyes stared, yet he seemed to see nothing. It was his *right* hand now that he clasped between his legs. He even wrinkled his face up once, and felt of it tenderly to show that it too was freezing. When the whole drama had become so painful that I thought I couldn't stand any more of it, Ekumiak suddenly straightened. With a theatrical pause, wherein he riveted our attention, his hand began to move. Almost imperceptibly, he was lifting up his clenched right fist. But he did not strike. He kept us waiting there with him, while the empathy that I myself felt in my muscles strained my back so much that I felt sore afterward. And then, suddenly, he struck. The suspense in the audience had been terrible. A great sigh went up from the Indians, as the hunter as last began to pull and pull and pull the imaginary body of the seal out of the water.

"Kosigwan" ("heavy"), growled out a deep Indian voice in tones of the most intense satisfaction.

It was accomplished. It was done. Then simply, in a pathetic gesture, Ekumiak knelt beside the seal for a moment and bowed his head and clasped his hands together. To my amazement, a tear was running down the cheek of one of the Indians. He had been *so* hungry! And now he was *so* thankful.

Rising, flushed with success, Ekumiak murmured something to Boyshish, still in fanciful and hysterical spirit.

"Now the seal is in his stomach!" cried Boyshish wildly, almost beside himself with pleasure, and all the other Indians loudly laughed. They really *laughed*. I could hardly believe it.

I took note of myself and of the whole scene. For 23 hours, Ekumiak had told us, an Eskimo used to sit waiting

171

for his seal. Twenty-three hours by the seal hole, without once leaving it! And we were going home tomorrow, from our warm tents—with nothing.

I went back to my tent and to sleep, somehow purged of those dreadful emotions that had beset all of us for the last few days. The situation had not changed, but I had. And so apparently had the Indians. The next morning Daniel brought us their decision; they would stay another 24 hours. We would all risk it for one more day.

KASAGEA! KASAGEA!

We really did not expect anything from one more day of hunting—not after so many days of nothing. But Doutt took a new lease on hope and proposed a new plan. On the twenty-third, he said, instead of giving up, we would split the party. He would stay with Daniel and Jacob Rupert, the best hunters, as long as the food lasted. The rest of us would get out as fast as we could to Clearwater Lake and our cache. It was agreed. We set out for our last day's hunt, almost but not entirely hopeless.

For three days past, the old dog had been tied up to our tent-flap, for Ekumiak had agreed that under the circumstances a dog could not be fed. Either the *kingmee* was already weak or he was remarkably obedient. He whined a little, but mostly he just slept. I used to suspect that the Eskimo might be saving bits from his own rations and feeding them to the dog, but if he did it, it was secretly.

Ekumiak's growing friendship for the Indians, brought to a fine climax with the drama in their tent the night before, was destroyed in an instant on the morning of the twenty-second. It was all too true that a little dog meat would have been greatly welcome. Daniel, on the morning of the twenty-second, passing by the sleeping *kingmee*, proposed to George with a laugh that we should eat him. Although Daniel's words were strange to Ekumiak, their meaning was unmistakable. From that moment on, Ekumiak again hated the Indians, and hated them with a hatred that was deadly and final.

The idea of eating the dog was not without virtue. Some explorers systematically plan to make their teams provide some of the rations, but it is far too utilitarian a plan for my stomach and is highly unfeasible in the land of Ekumiaks.

On this last day, each did whatever he thought best. Feeling that there was more hope of finding a supposed dead seal than of locating an entirely hypothetical live one, I persuaded Thomas George to mount upon a huge cake of floating ice, which we had chiselled from the main field, and there, holding one end of a long piece of fishing cord, to let us raft him about in the open water near where Daniel said he had killed the seal. An ice-chisel was Thomas George's guiding oar, and he poked about with it under the water hunting for the floating body of the *kasagea*.

It was an idyllic spot. Close to the Seal Lakes there were again good spruce trees, very low but thickly boughed and pretty. The sun had cleared many of them of snow, exposing the greenness. The little river came down at this spot over a rock ledge, forming an open rapids, the water separating at the foot of the rapids around a large island. Around this island, Thomas George went twisting and turning on his ice float, somewhat dangerously, it is true, but Thomas seemed only pleasantly excited. The faint spume and the splashing and the gurgle from the water filled both ears and eyes with charming music. I was very tired, so tired that it no longer hurt me when I thought about the Belchers—or so let us say—and yet I enjoyed myself after a fashion, all morning.

A loud-calling old cock ptarmigan felt the spring in the air as we felt it, and couldn't bear to take the moment calmly. He came presently near. Leaping up fifteen feet or more, beating his wings very rapidly together, his neck stretched forward almost to the breaking point, he would rise and then come fluttering straight down again onto the silvery snow. It was the first sign of the mating season. Melting snow showed faint patches upon the hill slopes, and flocks of rock ptarmigan were moving over them in vast numbers, feeding frantically on last summer's frozen berries just now beginning to be exposed.

The whole morning we poked, pried and peered ourselves weary, sending the Indian upon his chilling ice cake to hitherto inaccessible places in the large open water hole, trying to fathom the secrets of the dark rapids, trying to devise some means of finding the lost half-floating body of a seal. The dead seal would float near the surface. And suddenly, though I was actually watching the leaping ptarmigan at the moment, I was startled with an idea. The undercurrents might not be like those on the surface! If the current had not driven the seal down its obvious passage, then some obstruction within the water might be creating cross-currents that we could not see from above. A weighted cork was not much like a seal, but its progress should tell us something.

Unable to explain to the Indians, I simply abandoned the sampanning hunters and hurried back to camp where I got my cork and my weights and found Daniel Peta-cumeshcum. He came with me willingly, even without understanding, doubtless flattered when I led him once more back to the rapids where we still hunted for his own seal.

Weighting the cork until it sank sufficiently under the water, I played it out from the spot of the kill on some twenty feet of light line. We dug peep-holes to look through. The cork moved very slowly, straight down the main current as we had expected, while we kept the line loose and free. It drifted gently and lazily, but soon almost imperceptibly it began to sidle off to the right—over toward the river bank! We dug holes then, breathlessly, every few feet. And at last, without any tension whatever (for the line floated and bobbed on the surface of the water), the cork lay absolutely still. Perhaps a rock protruded from the river floor and created just back of it a protected spot? Whatever the cause, there was a pocket of stillness.

Daniel, cautiously digging out holes with his chisel, never once looked up. He seemed interminably slow. The cock ptarmigan on the shore was joined by another and they went leaping up together in a noisy duet. I could never again think of *kasagea* without seeing also the fluttering body of a ptarmigan. Daniel dug five peepholes in scarcely more minutes, trying to follow the hidden floating curve of the line. At the fifth hole, he was right over the cork! He made that hole larger then, while we all stared, hypnotized. I could scarcely breathe. Then he plunged downward with his longhandled chisel and touched the body below.

Daniel never lifted the chisel up—just stood there holding on to it, his mouth hanging open in shock and surprise. We knew then that he had found it. Both he and I were half-stunned. It was a yell from Thomas George that really shouted the tidings. Foolish grins, foolish talk, wild gestures from all of us. Good old Daniel, I thought! Good old George! Good old everybody! The natives and I kept on talking to one another because we just couldn't help it, and despite the strangeness of the words, there was no doubt in my mind of what they were saying. I looked around at the green-splashed, frosty shores of the river and the white sweeps of ice at our feet and at the pretty purling of the tumbling rapids, and it all seemed perfectly beautiful. Even finding the *kasagea* seemed the most natural thing in the world. The plan, the journey, the hunt, the specimen. Of course we had got our specimen. Men didn't go wandering around sub-Arctic mountains in the dead of winter for nothing.

As fast then as shaky legs would carry me, I got back to camp and rounded up the others. Jacob Rupert, who set out at once with the toboggan to help Daniel, was as pleased with our success as if he himself had got the seal, and the relief that showed on Doutt's face was reward enough. But Ekumiak was torn, I suspected, between shame and happiness—shame that he had not got his *five* seals yet and joy that at last there would be food for the *kingmee*.

Exactly what *kasagea* was would require many months, perhaps years, to determine, but certainly *kasagea* was not *netchek!** It was all that we needed to know to make us wildly, almost entirely happy.

We had the strange skin, all that we needed for our specimen, and the natives had the meat. It was a situation that worried Ekumiak. It is Eskimo who live on seals. Indians are bird-eaters! Indians are fish-eaters! In great indignation, he explained to everyone in our tent that this thing was not a bird or a fish. It was a seal. And since it was a seal, and he was the Inuk, he thought he had better be having a little of it. Despite his hatred of Daniel, which now included all the other Indians, Ekumiak went off self-righteously just before supper to the natives' tent. He swallowed his pride and displayed new cunning. He said a prayer of thanksgiving; he sang hymns of gratitude; he smiled and listened and sat expectantly with the Indians in their feasting circle, until he had got a little seal meat, on the side.

What an evening! The *kasagea* was a female. It had in its womb a seven-and-a-half-pound foetus. Two specimens in one! Tomorrow, Ekumiak boasted when he came back with a full stomach, he would make the *kudlu* for us—the seal-oil lamp. It was seal oil, he assured George sagely, that a man really needed to do his writing.

A red fox smelled our kill and ranged all night about the lake and river barking. With the wind up for days, he too had been hungry. The Indian hunters, all of whom had insisted that *kasagea* didn't eat in the winter, found the well-filled stomach of our specimen inexplicable. The

*The scientific report on *kasagea* (such as must always precede any popular description) has not yet been published. [The scientific report was published in 1942. See J. Kenneth Doutt, "A Review of the Genus *Phoca*," *Annals of the Carnegie Museum*, XXIX (1942-43), 61-125—Editor.]

seal had been dining on Arctic char. Two Indians who had gone up the lake many miles distant, in order to hunt without frightening the possible seals with their guns, came back late at night all worn out and with only six little birds. They looked at the pile of fresh meat as if it were the end of everything—the golden dawn of the missionaries' Heavenly Day!

The Eskimos on the coast, Ekumiak now told us, had jeered at him for wanting to come along, for he would not be able, they said, to hunt *kasagea*. *Kasagea*, they said, did not blow at holes. And in a way, the coast Inuit had been right.

Doutt on the last day had been arriving at important conclusions. *Kasagea* did not need blow-holes on the main surface, for there was plenty of air underneath the shore ledges that surrounded the Seal Lake on all sides and banked also the northerly rivers. The first freeze-up comes suddenly. The autumn waters are still swift and deep. The streams freeze over from side to side in a single night, and the shore ice, being attached and stronger, retains its original position even after the centre ice has broken, floated away, refrozen, broken and so on, until the sinking water has finally permanently frozen all the way across. Under the jutting, suspended ledges of early ice, *kasagea* can come "to blow at the holes," protected from the wind, even climbing out of the water and resting on rocks or under-ledges, never revealing himself to anybody. Little wonder that the natives never did any winter killing of *kasagea*. Little wonder that they were loath to come in the first place to such an unnatural hunting ground.

When the inlanders hunt *kasagea* in summer, they lie in ambush and shoot those animals that come to sun on shore. Eleven were once taken in a group, it is said, all sleeping at the edge of a shallow. The few wounded that escaped into the water sank so near land that the bodies were recovered.

Only Jacob Rupert still had faith in the old ways common to all before the coming of the guns. Few Ungava natives nowadays can make a seal net and few have ever seen it used. Jacob Rupert's grandfather had been a famous seal-net hunter, and Jacob is the only one of all the Indians I have met who makes the old fabled hours of silence and suffering any more than a fine tradition. But the old skills are of little use now, for gun sounds frighten all animals and make them unnaturally nervous and wary, so that however the old ways used to be, they can no longer be depended upon. The old ways mean suffering. The gun ways seem easy. But the guns will destroy all the hunting eventually, both by depleting the game and by causing it to migrate. New homes are legion in the sub-Arctic, and all the Arctic North lies free to be lived in. While the Ungava hunter continues to hunt with the gun, more and more often he will come home emptyhanded.

On the very next day after he recovered the first one, Daniel Petacumeshcum brought in another seal. Living on the meat of the two already killed, the Indians stayed on willingly for five more days, but I did nothing further to help in the hunt. Released from the anxiety of our returning empty-handed, my mind could be given entirely to the study of birds. The snow, the spruces, the isolation, the hours alone among the thickets and snow-drifts, induced thronging memories of my childhood in Alberta. One early morning, as George rattled the pans over the stove and the hoarfrost still lay heavy on the canvas of my sleeping-bag, I waked, transfixed by the thrilling song of the pine grosbeak—the *seekookalillu* of the Eskimos.

It was the first time I had heard one in the Seal Lakes region and I half-thought I must be dreaming. It was just as in the old days: "Hear that?" I thought Frank Farley was saying, as he used to say when he was a man of 50 and I a boy of fourteen. "Hear that? A flock of pine grosbeak just ahead!" Each Saturday of that year, Frank and I walked the six miles to Battle River, and I had carried the gun because it was lighter than Mrs. Farley's food baskets. (The gun, however, was only a gesture. Farley wouldn't have thought of using it.)

The birds were always pressed for food in winter, near Battle River. Blue jays and hairy woodpeckers scuttled through the high branches, wanting to come down. Chickadees flipped around us almost into the fire, alighting on our hands if we didn't keep them moving, standing gratefully on top of Farley's ear whenever he would take his hat off. (They were more friendly than these Hudsonian chickadees and had more buzz to their song.)

"Now don't pick up that wood from the ground," Farley would remind me sternly, "and watch out for that food basket! Ethel made us a pie today!" He was always saying how bully the tea tasted. "This stuff would float a monkeywrench! But drink it, boy! Drink it! That'll grow hair on your chest!"

The smell of ham as it fried, the big soft slices of Ethel's homemade bread spread thickly with Ethel's homemade jelly . . . and a grosbeak always singing. . . .

"Come and get it," George broke in on me rudely, and I scrambled for my bag and tardily into my pants trying to get a look at the retreating *seekookalillu*. But it had disappeared over the hill. Across the way, an Indian was coming from the tent, his brown face reminding me sharply that it was Ungava. It was *not* Battle River.

After *kasagea*, there was no more piemaking or any chumminess in the evening. I did nothing in the day but walk and walk and nothing in the evening but write about it. The Indians had eaten themselves sick on the seal meat, and Ekumiak had made us a seal-oil lamp from the *ooksook*. We could read papers tonight, he told George, sighing happily as we stared in admiration at the tin piepan of oil with a soppy cloth for a wick, from which came (along with smoke and stinks) a soft, yellow

179

and charming light.

However unsuited he was for the trail and the *kasagea* hunt, we could not find it in our hearts to be sorry that we had taken Ekumiak with us. He was like a pet chickadee in our tent. Seeing him always busy, eager, uncomplaining, watching his tender solicitude for the old dog, we were better able to endure our darkest times. For Ekumiak is the kind of person who sometimes convinces the most cynical philosophers of the eventual good ending of all things.

INDIANS OF CLEARWATER ISLAND

Food had acted on the old dog like wine. When at last we started off for Richmond Gulf again, he whined, he trembled, he cocked his ears like a jack-rabbit and waved his tail like a strenuous flag. I never saw more violent joy in any dog. He nearly ran the legs off George and Ekumiak.

All along the way the willow ptarmigan were showing signs of spring. The males, barking and croaking as they warmed up for the mating season, were flecked with brown about the head and neck and strutted upon every bare tundra knoll—natural platforms for their exhibitions—flying up with necks extended before the crowds of busy, disinterested females. But without response their shows would not long continue, and often the males too would be found quietly feeding with the females on the blueberries, bearberries and cranberries that were everywhere beginning to be exposed. The sun grew daily brighter, and the snow more soft and wet. It was the last day of March when we finally left the east bank of Clearwater Lake, taking a course due west[14] across the sloppy snow-covered ice toward the one Indian teepee on the lake's largest island.

This Clearwater Lake Island of the interior country was on the very edge of the tundra, and showed perfectly the merging of bushland and barrens. Two rocky peaks soared above a deep valley, cupped within rocks and knolls and with only the north end open to the lake. It was 5:30 in the afternoon with the sun still visible when we reached the edge of the island. Fishing-poles were suspended over dozens of holes chopped out of the ice, each surrounded with its circular spruce-bough wind-break. A single large teepee made up the whole encampment. It stood in the calm spring evening light under a crimsoned sky, the rocky brown peaks shining above it and the white and green slopes closing it around, a sort of old grey bird-nest among the trees.

Fourteen people lived in this one teepee—Jimmie Miamiamiskow, his wife, their three children, Jacob Rupert, his wife, their five children, the old chief (Rupert's father) and a widowed young woman.

Ceremoniously, even though it was near dark and camp-making should have been done, Daniel Petacumeshcum delivered us to the proud old man who sat at one end of the teepee on his grey, dirty and lousy blanket, while all the Richmond Gulf Indians kissed every member of the Clearwater teepee—men, women and children. I was weary, and like Ekumiak's old dog, almost frantic for home. The heat from the blistering stove (a converted gasoline drum), the crowds, the slow and pompous solemnity with which presentations were made, the dreadful stink of bodies, tobacco and fish, irritated me beyond measure. But the visit to the teepee is something that any stranger at Clearwater Lake in Ungava must endure.

Many birds were crying outside, even though it was so near sunset. The jays at the fishbone heap by the door of the teepee had scarcely moved away at all as we came in. The rock ptarmigan's lonely croakings came in faint echoes from surrounding hills. (A flock of over a hundred birds had passed us at the edge of the island.) I longed to be free. I felt wronged, and scornful of all Indians, even of Jacob Rupert who was admirable in almost every way. I yearned to have our inland journey finished, to climb the steep slope of the Gulf hill still so many miles beyond us, to see the dogs fly before the now lightly loaded *komatik* faster than they had ever flown before, to come at last in sight of Great Whale River and learn what our fate was to be. Was it still possible to cross the ice bridge to the Belchers? My mind played an endless record of the question.

How I yearned, as I sat in the squalid Indian teepee, to be back in my own *tooktoo*—as the east-coast Eskimos called the gabled tents. In our own tent George would not talk much, understanding why I was an ill-natured, frankly weary man. Doutt seldom talked, and Ekumiak never, except in a crisis or unless he were encouraged. Our tent was neat and airy and we were never much in each other's way. The fourteen relatives lining both sides of the teepee sat cross-legged on their dirty blankets making an aisle up to the throne-blanket where the chieftain sat. The chief spoke once, but his words were not scintillating: *"Oochimakanni,"* he said, meaning "I (literally "me") chief!" On the empty space allotted to us on the blankets we had to sit stolidly until Daniel Petacumeshcum finally concluded that it was time for us to go.

The women did not stay with us long. Rising without a word they slipped almost bodiless, one by one, out of the teepee, each wearing a big dark Government shawl and carrying a length of sealskin cord for hauling in the wood for the night. They had probably chopped it that afternoon.

When at last we were leaving, a little girl of ten or twelve returned from the fishing-holes, swinging along on her little round showshoes, carrying two trout, one of about five pounds and the other ten. Craving the taste of something not canned or dried or cured, we asked George to make arrangements for a food exchange. For our beans, flour, tea and sugar the Clearwater Indians gladly supplied all our hunting party with plenty of char such as the child had been carrying.

182

A woman came to our tent to complete the trade. She was young, but alas not pretty. Over a calico dress, which flapped in the wind about her skinny shanks, she wore a dark-blue man's sweater and a shawl on her head. Snaky trails of oily black hair hung tangled and neglected almost to her waist. She was small and flat, and like all the other Clearwater Island women, very, very thin.

In a food shortage, among most Hudson Bay Indians, the girl children are first to be denied. Starvation days follow a traditional routine. The grown hunters always take precedence until the food supply is nearly out. Then only the little boys, the hunters of the future, continue to be fed. Thus it was that Boyshish, who was only eight years old at the time, survived the winter of starvation that killed the 21 Indians in the Seal Lakes region in 1930. How Luk Cashe survived, I never dared to inquire.

Most Indian women show the results of early starvations. The bony hands of the girl with the fish clasped the handle of the heavy pail that she held directly in front of her. They were less like hands than like sharp birds' feet; the skin was frostbitten, windblacked and crusty with dirt. George thanked her with a cheerful word, and at the sound of it she raised her thin coppery face and beady glittering eyes to his for a startled moment, and then, without answering, swung swiftly away.

We had the fish for supper, six or seven large, grey-green and silver-flecked Arctic char of about seven pounds each, with faintly pinkish flesh, rich, moist and delicate. We would have nothing else on the table. Our Indians, who had been hunting ptarmigan that day as we came along, let the birds wait while their fish simmered slowly in two large pails of boiling water.

We commented on the fact that Jacob Rupert was not the only Clearwater Indian to wear the Good Hunter's insignia. Every man in the place was wearing it, by which I judged that necessity in the interior made every hunter an expert. Perhaps the reason there was but one teepee at Clearwater Lake was that these few really skilled marksmen adequately covered all the vast wild territory that lay about.

That night the melting continued in alarming proportions. At seven o'clock a very wet snow began to fall, clinging to the tent roofs half an inch deep all over, melting along the ridgepole and running down through the spark-burnt holes of our Indians' shelter in little rivers. In our tent moisture permeated the air and we sat down to supper with drops running down our cheeks and noses. Before we had finished eating we had to cover our floor, the sleeping-bags and all the equipment with tarpaulins. We rushed through the last of the meal. It was awful. Supper over, we got out of our clothes and stuck them under the edge of the tarpaulins, discovered our sleeping-bags in the floor confusion, and crawled into them somehow. I pulled the tarps up under my chin and settled down at last, weary but excited, to listen to the drip and flow of the world outside. It was scarcely eight o'clock, but there was nothing we could possibly do except, as Ekumiak suggested, *"sini-look-ta"* ("everybody sleep").

On our second day at Clearwater Lake Island, heavy fog obscured the early morning. The air was still. The temperature rose and kept on rising until it was 38 degrees above zero. By ten o'clock the fog was gone and the sun shone brilliantly. Potential flood threatened all our party. Perhaps, George suggested, we should abandon the equipment and the specimens and go down in canoes when the Clearwater Indians went out to the Bay for their summer encampment? (No-one could ever be quite certain whether or not George was joking!) What would we not have given for a biting wind that day, a scouring blast of a good ground-drifter, to turn all that sop and flow and splash into a bleak, white, icy waste once more!

Before noon, at the invitation of the old chief, George and I waded out through the slush to one of the fishing-holes at the edge of the island to take our chances at fishing. Before we reached the hole, a mile and a half from our tent, we had accepted everything just as it was, the sun simply as a sun and the warmth as warmth; we let ourselves almost be glad to see the spring.

Around the fishing-hole was the usual circle of boughs, stuck upright into the ice and frozen there in a close green shield to protect the fishermen from wind. And within the circle was a brushpile seat, five or six inches high and wide enough so that George and I both could sit upon it and have room to pull our feet up onto it also. The day was balmy and the sky filled with drifting clouds. There was a kind of sweetness in the light. Snow-packed paths made by the women and children only, in their half-size snowshoes, led from the island out to each hole in the lake and also from one hole to another. Forty or fifty holes, with lines suspended on a stick, above them, were rigged in such a way that the stick would drop when-ever a fish took the bait. The women could tell even from a distance when to come and get it. But some women now sat waiting behind the wind-breaks as we did, holding the poles in their hands. George and I fished as the women did when they were in a hurry, temptingly jiggling our lines up and down. The Clearwater Lake Indians had been entirely out of shells most of that winter, according to Jacob, and had lived without food of any kind except fish and a few uncovered berries.

Heedless of men, the rock and willow ptarmigan were out in great numbers, remarkably tame and unafraid. I listened to the pleading of the willow birds as they called to and answered one another. The rattling cry of the rockers echoed from the encircling tundra plateaus above us and from the sloping hillsides. It was a time of great agitation on the island among both birds and people, for the thaw-opened slopes of lichen, with their fine "refrigerated" berries, were being gradually exposed; the birds talked incessantly about it, but the feelings of the taciturn Indians could only be surmised.

From my seat on the brushpile, I could look up and see

into a tundra meadow, where in one place a male rock ptarmigan took a long and craning survey of the territory and then gave two short, low chuckles. From under wind-twisted low spruces came two other males just like him. The·three cocks then ran across the mottled ground to the nearest patch of exposed greenness and there began pecking up the thawing berries. In orderly increase, like drilling soldiers, birds moved group by group out from under the spruces, until the whole hillside at last was alive with quietly feeding ptarmigan, all astutely following the original leader. Hundreds had come in a very little while to feed on the slope, but not a one had so much as raised a wing. Meeting a snowbank, the flock would become temporarily invisible, but as by magic would startlingly reappear when their whiteness was once more thrown into contrast with the light green of the next patch of cladonia. Twelve red-polls flew over, swift and wild. At the very edges of the lake where the heavily seeded andropogan grew, many birds ravenously clustered right to the very tip of the stiffish stalk and with skilful contortions extricated even the seeds that lay under their very feet. The stalks, often bending over under the weight, would still be clung to by the tenacious birds who always kept on pecking and eating. Thomas George and Luk Cashe, working their way on a bird hunt up the southeast hillside, eventually rested, outlined like two statues high upon the ridge-crest. Suddenly Thomas George, sharply marked against the sky, raised his gun, and we heard his shot in a moment echoing across the still valley.

"Gosh," cried George suddenly, "I got a bite!" He gave a swift up-jerk. But in vain. The bait was gone. The fish was gone—and doubtless laughing to itself already far below us, in some fishy controlled-by-currents way. Then for the first time in all our hardships together, George displayed temper. He was peevish, even sullen. Fishing, I judged, was a vital matter to George—possibly more vital than the terrors of solitude or the imminence of death. I was having the same experience but without George's reactions.

"To blazes!" cried George at last, in a great huff. "Darn fools won't bite anyway!" For George-the-mild, it was practically profanity. An Indian woman, passing us on the trodden path between the holes, looked our way suspiciously at George's alien outburst.

She was a youngish woman, I judged by her hipline and from her exceedingly rapid gait. Perhaps already she had tracked all over the island (which was five miles or so long), but even at this hour she was still "swift as a hawk in flight." She was dark, sallow, dispirited in body, seemingly as mutilated and beaten as a twisted Ungava tree in the uplands. But like the trees, I thought, she would be long-enduring. Her bronzed hue, her colourless lips, her dark, expressionless eyes, her angular frame, her silence, her suspicions—all made her typical of the race. There was nothing picturesque about any of the Clear-water Lake inhabitants except as windstripped tree trunks are picturesque. In the long black wool Government coat and huge black shawl, this lank little body was a dreary sight, but had not the silly-looking calico dress printed with pale pink rosebuds been hanging below her dark coat like a ridiculous ruffle around the legs of a raven, she would have had a kind of tragic fitness for Ungava and her life. As it was, she seemed pitiful and unappealing—merely poor.

She sat down at the fishing-hole adjoining ours, some distance away. With motionless stoicism she held her body rigid, resting one arm on one bony knee as she squatted, moving her hand from the wrist only, jiggling the line in small but very rhythmic motion, up-and-down, up-and-down. From under her dress protruded the tan caribou-hide feet of her winter moccasins with the whitish knee-length canvas legs slightly showing.

What an occasion it must have been for that lonely island to have any visitors—even native ones. Whether pleasant or unpleasant, certainly the presence of strangers was a momentous thing, and yet, as we left our place, passing close by her, the Indian woman never even looked up.

It rained throughout our third night at Clearwater Lake Island except for an interval near four o'clock in the morning when the old dog cut the temporary quiet with dismal howls. He refused to be comforted and the whole encampment had to listen until daylight. The lake was thick and grey with the melted snow upon its surface— like a soupy sea. And one of us, let him be nameless, discovered that he was lousy. There were lice in his clothes, his bedding and even in his mitts. It was the last straw!

We fought back as best we could, using what flit we had brought along and making careful daily inspections, tormented every minute by creepings real and imaginary, painfully controlling an almost constant desire to scratch. We had always known that our own Indian helpers had lice, and at last George asked Ekumiak jokingly if he (Ekumiak) had them too, to which the Inuk answered politely with a grave and simple *"Ah"* ("Yes"). All Eskimos had them, he went on to explain to George, around Great Whale River.

Three jays flitted about camp all day, but I was unable to trail them through the slush to see whether or not they were nesting. After a trout dinner at noon, I went off after some red-polls, and although I eventually lost them, I had a good walk. Keeping of necessity to high rocky ground, I found a place from which I could view almost the whole island. It was less than a mile wide, four or five miles long, and lay north to south. Cliffs rose 200 feet high or more, and on top of them were high rolling plateaus of climax tundra. Although most rocks seemed to be of granite, there was a preponderance of reddish streaking in the cliffs, indicating considerable iron. Cladonia was the dominant plant, forming a climax tundra on both rocks and gravel, accompanied by Arctic willow, Labrador tea, blueberry, cranberry and crowberry shrubs, all shrubs lying in the more moist places, where I found also spagnum and baked-apple plants. As a sub-climax, black spruces were not uncommon in the moisture, tamaracks grew in a few places near muskegs and ponds, and on the sand and gravel climax ridges, a few sedges and andropogans flourished.

Not only did the island reveal both treeland and tundra on its surface, but with both willow and rock ptarmigan living there in numbers, the birds too were shown neatly in contrast. Both species roosted at night in the snow-banks under the spruces, but the willow ptarmigan kept to the forests and thickets as much as possible, feeding chiefly on willow shrubs and never lured very far upon the hill slopes even by berries, while the rock ptarmigan spent only the stormy days in the lowlands and could be found from sunrise to sunset feeding on the highest of the berry-covered heights. I saw rock ptarmigan commonly sunning on the cladonia slopes, and sometimes on the very tops of the highest cliffs. Our Indians shot eighteen rock ptarmigan on their hilltop hunt that day, and when I examined the stomachs I found that the birds had all fed exclusively on blueberries. Four of the cocks (who get very brown in summer) showed two or three really dark brown feathers on their necks and backs. It was a clear announcement of the arrival of spring.

Clearwater Lake Island was a fine spot for academic study, but my pleasure in it was much diminished by the memory of my morning visit to the Indians' teepee. Doutt and I had been called to the big teepee right after breakfast to look at sickly George Rupert, the old chief, Jacob Rupert's brother.[15] There was no longer any show of pride in the teepee or any ceremony. George Rupert sat on the floor on his blankets and obviously suffered. We decided that he probably had kidney stones, but we knew of nothing that might relieve him. We hated to advise him that he would have to bear his pain until August, five months more, and then get himself to the coast to meet the doctor's boat when it put in at Great Whale River. Knowing something about the great pain of kidney stones, I avoided looking at the sufferer while George translated our verdict.

It was a sad morning, indeed. Freed from ceremonial strain, we could observe the other inhabitants of the teepee. *All* of Jacob Rupert's children had tuberculosis. One had a badly affected hip, and the others, who according to Jacob were running daily fevers, were diseased in the lungs apparently. Even while we stood waiting by George Rupert's pallet, Jacob's youngest boy was seized with a fit of coughing and he spat a mucous so red that it looked like nothing but blood, dripping down upon the floor of green spruce boughs and running under them onto the white snow. Jimmie Miamiamiskow's daughter had a bad cough along with a sore chest, and she too, Jacob said, had been spitting.

There was little hope for the Clearwater Indians, I thought miserably, living as they did in such close association. Their frequent starvations left them little resistance. Even the hunters, out all day and constantly exercising, would probably contract the disease eventually. There were penalties in a simple life; the twisted-tree of a woman whom we had watched at the fishing-hole would not, after all, be very long-enduring.

I remembered the fine physiques of the free-roaming hunters who came often to the post and realized that they gave a false impression. The treeline Indians were not actually healthy and vigorous people. I looked with new eyes at the solemn faces in the teepee and at the red blood bright on the boughs.

All in all, we wasted four days at the island in Clearwater Lake. On the night of April 1, the southwest wind increased until there was a swift gale blowing, pulling strongly at our tent that we had thought pitched in a well-protected spot. The temperature dropped; it soon read 30 above zero. We gathered about for supper, listening with smiles to the moaning and whining of that fine cold hard-freezing wind, the kind of wind to clear the land and the lake of slush and give us back the hard whiteness of the trail. Even the old Indian from the Clearwater teepee who came over to do his nightly begging for tobacco, or moccasins, or ammunition, or food, and especially for our promise that we would leave food at his son's camp, which was farther on toward the Gulf—even the beggar did not irritate us. We sent him off kindly, and he went muttering his usual Indian equivalent of "there is no harm in asking."

The next morning we were up by daylight prepared to start, but when the Indians felt the force of the gale, they refused to travel in it. Twelve miles of open lake lay in our immediate path. Daniel argued violently that the storm was a blizzard and that no-one could travel. We demanded to start off at once, come what may. But at last we went with the Indians to a hill to test the force of the drifter and there discovered that we could scarcely stand up in it. *"Hematugan nonnon abatstwn!"* cried one of the Indians in excitement, holding up the cloth that we might see the thinness of his parka. *"Awasha tekayon!"* ("too cold!") they all said. And so for one more day, although the ground was white and glassy hard again, we waited in camp in the Clearwater Island valley.

But finally, on April 3, at six o'clock in the morning, we left. The old dog was in another frenzy of delight. The slightly rough ice on the lake offered almost perfect resistance to the lightly loaded toboggans and we took off fast, all in high spirits.

Daniel Petacumeshcum's toboggan had had something added, a new pair of snowshoes made by the old chief of the Clearwater teepee. They were undeniably beautiful, with big bright-red wool tassels outlining the points at the back and a few scattered tassels decorating the edges. A whole row of tiny tassels outlined the tips of the toes. I never saw Daniel wear them; perhaps he only bought the shoes to sell for *mishanagen* (or "put-on-paper,"

191

meaning credit at the store), or perhaps he simply would not be the only man of our party to wear snowshoes with such bright new tassels, but I am sure he gloated over the precious purchase all the way home. All the other hunters were waiting assembled and stared, of course, envious and awestruck, when Daniel placed the neat package on top of his load. He had wrapped the shoes in a white flour-sacking, and they rode before us all the way to the Gulf, proud symbol of Daniel's yearnings and vanity.

We soon reached the first cache beyond Clearwater Lake Island, but we found that it had been raided, and when we reached the Richmond Gulf cache, we discovered that it had been raided too. The settlement at Richmond Gulf was still in an uproar from the excitement of the robbery. The women had done it. They admitted the theft defiantly. Their men were gone, they said, and they had been hungry!

We had learned of the death of Luk Cashe's sister even before we reached Richmond Gulf settlement because of a little tree that we found by the trail. It was the *death-news tree*, felled, and then buried upside down with the bushy end in the snow; the trunk end stood topmost and was supported by a stick beneath it. The Indians had hurried forward at the sight, and with set faces had read the blazed news. Then they had all wept and grieved for perhaps five minutes, and afterward seemed quite cheerful again.

Had the tree contained news that was interesting but not important, it would have been set into the snow with the bushy end upward, but leaning out at a very sharp angle. This method of signalling news to all passers-by is known on the treeline as the "moccasin-telegraph," and it relays information with remarkable efficiency.

Beyond Richmond Gulf, George, Doutt and I were alone again, on our way back to the Great Whale River Post with Ekumiak, another Eskimo driver, the dogs and the *komatik*.

At the top of the big hill out of Richmond Gulf,

Ekumiak looked back at the Cairn Island teepees, back over the hills and the once mysterious rolling miles of green and silver inlands, and then he spat out his final syllables on the matter. There were weeks of fear and injustice and regret in his voice: *"Adelay pingatu!"* ("The Indians are no good!")

The Indians had never understood the relation between Ekumiak and his dog. If there are Eskimos who beat their dogs to death, Ekumiak would not acknowledge kinship with them. He would say they do not belong among the Tuseerukoo, the Eskimos who live or hunt near Richmond Gulf. I doubt that they even belong on Hudson Bay *tuckimo* meaning Hudson Bay east shore, "where-the-moon-gets-up." To an Eskimo on Hudson Bay east shore, a dog is not only the symbol of man's prosperity; it is the symbol of life itself. When Daniel the Indian said *"meetsu"* ("eat"), and pointed with an index finger at the *kingmee*, that was beyond forgiveness. There had been an incident on Clearwater Island, moreover, that was almost worse.

One night, while we were waiting on the island for the slush to freeze over, the Indians had secretly borrowed the dog to haul a toboggan for them and they had not brought him back. Ekumiak didn't believe that they had simply lost the *kingmee*, and all of us in our tent had doubts. Perhaps they had murdered him and dropped his body into a water hole. They still hated the dog for the food he had eaten. They were Indians, and Ekumiak was an Eskimo! That was what we really thought the trouble. To conceal his hurt, no doubt, Ekumiak loudly demanded that the Indians should pay him the credit equivalent of fifteen dollars. Then the Indians got busy! The *kingmee* was found in less than an hour. He had entered the island at the wrong end among the hills and forests, and there, frightened and running away in the night, the dog had got his lines entangled among the trees and bushes and been held a prisoner. When the Indians found him and brought him safely to Ekumiak, the toboggan still dragged disconsolately after him. But Ekumiak had been more wrought up than ever. *"Adelay pingatu!"* he had told them then, and now he said it again, bringing to a close his strange and wonderful journey.

He had not learned to love his neighbours the Indians, but he had come to understand them a little—perhaps better than any other Eskimo on the whole Bay east coast. He had lived down a great fear. He would never again be only a happy, naïve, superstitious little Inuk. He had met something larger than the seal hunt or the church service. He had had an adventure with his own soul.

I think Ekumiak rode back every step of the way from Richmond Gulf to Great Whale River. I see him yet, his fat indignant little body sitting sidewise on the loaded *komatik*, his pudgy legs stuck straight out in front of him determinedly jutting from the side of the sled, his round brown oily nose just showing its tip beyond the ring of dog fur that encircled his profile. His round shoulders and short-necked body curved there on the load in a soft huddle like a fat letter *C*. He never dismounted, regardless of the occasion.

Once in a while the other Eskimo driver, subordinate in authority and possibly out of awe for this Eskimo Ulysses who had seen the dark regions of the Indians' land, would jump off the sled to shove it sidewise and avoid hitting a rock or an ice chunk. The rest of us rode a little, and walked when necessary—that is, most of the time.

We got home from the Seal Lakes in six days of travelling and four of waiting at Clearwater Island, on the flood and the wind. Coming home, we covered in less than a week the same distance it had taken us five weeks to cover when going in with the loaded toboggans. By the time we got back to Great Whale River, I had ruined two good pairs of deerskin boots such as would have lasted the ordinary native for many a season. Although we had gone into the interior, as the crow flies, only about 150 miles, we had actually walked almost 500.

My specimens from Ungava, I did not have time to skin out while we were in the interior; the cold preserved them until I could care for them many weeks later. I put them at night into my big fibre collecting case just as they were, where they remained for days fortunately frozen solid. I had, of course, stuffed up all the birds' throats, immediately after retrieving them, with a tiny wad of absorbent cotton, lest blood should spill out of the throat upon the feathers. Since I could not get at the collecting case while we were on the trail, I had to lay my freshest specimens underneath the canvas top cover of a toboggan until we camped each night, pointing out the position of the body to everyone and making it clear in all dialects that *no-one was to let himself sit down* upon that spot!

BIG TALK IN A BARBER SHOP

It was early evening but still light when we came in sight of Great Whale River Post. The dogs raced like mad for that last half-mile, while we hung on fast and hoped the sled wouldn't hit a rock. It was a flashy and deceptive end to our journey. The dogs never ran like that for anything but the sight of the post-house, the sight of a seal or the sniff of human excrement. Drooping as a tired Husky dog often seems, he will still always have speed held for the home-stretch or the hunting emergency. Our driver had to jump off the sled and crowd the dogs into a circle to make them stop short of the high radio lying on the ground, being repaired by the two white men who crouched over it.

We had swept in grandly over the snows amidst the barking of excited dogs, but we met a non-committal stare from the Scottish very blue eyes of the stranger and an undeniably cold glare from our once good friend Ross. As it happened, I got to them first.

"You must be Bob Cruickshank," I said, for we had

already had word on the trail that the manager of the Belcher Island Post was still waiting for Doutt and me on the mainland. My pulse was beating fast. I could scarcely wait to blurt out the question. Could we still chance the crossing? Was it possible that he still expected us to go? But I was too embarrassed by the anger on Ross' face to inquire directly. "I suppose you thought we were never coming," I hedged, smiling at Ross in a way that must have looked sheepish.

"This is Twomey," Ross told Cruickshank in a grudging voice.

"Well, I figured you might be lost," Cruickshank admitted, still not smiling, "way up there." He glanced vaguely toward the inland distance with a look that for all its casual disinterestedness was somehow young and eager.

"You fellows must have had every Indian in the hills working for you!" broke in Ross bitterly as if unable to contain his wrath any longer. "What did you think would happen to my furs in the meantime?"

So that was it, I suddenly realized with relief. Of course, we had been selfish. Ross had a right to be angry, and I simply got out from under.

"You'd better ask Doutt about that," I answered as Doutt joined us, and then I fled.

Ross greeted Doutt with a sour face and a sarcastic cheerfulness.

"You did a fine job of clearin' me outta Indians, didn't you!" the manager began.

"Couldn't help it," explained Doutt shortly. "We had to have them too!"

That was all there was to it. Very little, really. But life would never again be quite so rosy for us in the little house where Ross lives at the mouth of the Great Whale River.

Leaving the unfriendly fur men, Doutt and I went on into the house to clean ourselves up. Warmth; easy-chair, with dark old tapestry upholstery on it; Ross' chair; a day couch; the big rocking-chair—which Doutt dropped into. We looked around in relief and comfort. In a house again! It was late afternoon, windless and still, with a very clear light coming in from the southwest window. We looked over the mouth of the river and over the pressure ice onto the Bay, which had taken on a clear yellowish glow with the quiet sunset.

We had entered through the kitchen and found Mary Took-a-Look with a whisky bottle in her hand, using it to roll out some piecrust on her little dough board. With a shy grin she shook hands with both of us, but we didn't try to talk. She was fixing warm wash-water in the big white pitcher for us to take upstairs and setting out the white tin washpan. We'd had a glimpse of the dinner— canned roast beef (a special treat to us), with fresh potatoes (brought from Moose Factory by Mary Took-a-Look's lover). We listened to the sounds of everything and smelled the odours of everything, and were through with the trail for life!

That night, after a round or two of further argument, Ross thawed out again and we all began talking. Cruickshank in the meantime prepared to cut off my hair. (Doutt had decided to hang on to his.) Everyone at Great Whale River had lately been sick.

"You want to watch out," Ross warned us seriously. "The man on the mail sled brought a cold up with him and we've all had it. You know what that means up here." Ross was still sore in the muscles of his back. Young Jeff was away. He had been so ill that a native had sledded him down toward Moose Factory. The sled had been gone for a month and no-one knew what had happened.

"We had to get him out of here while there was still time," Ross said, worried; "it looked to me like appendicitis." There probably wouldn't be any word about Jeff until August, for sledding time was practically over. Obviously it was very risky to cross the ice to the Belchers, but Cruickshank said determinedly that cross we would, if

197

the rest of us could keep our chins up. Bob had brought in a kitchen chair and tied Mary Took-a-Look's apron around my neck.

"I'm the barber," he explained professionally. "Best thing up here," he continued, as he suddenly grabbed up a hank of my unruly hair, with a loud snip, "is just to get rid of it!" He himself was almost as bald as an egg, from a very close cropping. Then he held up for display the seven or eight long black curls that had collected on the back of my neck. They looked like some little girl's, and even the quiet George let out a fine haw-haw. Bob amused the crowd for a while by cutting a plaid design on the top of my head. Then he brought me Ross' little mirror. I frightened myself. My face was almost black from the wind and was blotched all over from frostbite and cold blisters. My beard was black and thick and three or four inches long. Even Ross forgot his "mad" for the moment, for with my plaid top crowning the rest of me, I was startling to behold.

Ross and Bob had endless questions about the country and the seal, and we had a lot of questions too. Was Boyshish really conjuring one night when we had heard him singing in an endless chant to the snow-blind Indians, on those dark days in the Seal Lakes region? No, said Ross; it was quite probable that Boyshish was imitating the seal song of the old conjurers, but that he did not himself believe. A few men living near Great Whale River do still chant the otter, the seal and the beaver songs, in which the priest or conjurer supposedly converses with the conjurer-god, but the true conjuror of the old days was evidently a ventriloquist — for two separate conversing voices could always be heard. At Neoskweskau 300 miles up the Rupert River where Ross was once stationed, there used to be much conjuring, and always when Ross' modern Neoskweskau Indians came to a rapids they always sang the rapids song.

Ross believed that our Indian helpers were not Ungava tribe Indians, but belonged instead to the northern-most tribes of the Eastern Crees.[16] When we spoke of the death-tree and the moccasin-telegraph, Ross told tales of death at Neoskweskau, where the Indians heap tobacco on a beloved's grave and give canoes to the dead. He told about one old Indian husband who gave up every blanket from his teepee for the grave of his wife, leaving none at all for himself, although it was in dead winter.

An Eskimo woman from the Gulf had visited Great Whale River for only one day, Ross remembered, when we asked about the Arctic throat infection. She had arrived seeming perfectly well, but she had died of the throat infection on that same day.

"We always hate to see the mailman, or to see the boat come," said Ross. "An epidemic of some kind is sure to follow." I thought that I remembered reading in Admiral Byrd's records that his men caught cold just from opening some new packing-cases.

"If you catch any polar bears over on the Belchers," said Ross, "remember that the livers are poisonous. Eskimos won't feed bear liver even to dogs. Seal livers are okay if the seals are young ones, but the livers of old seals cause jaundice. Neither Indians nor dogs can eat weasels, because frightened weasels spray their stinking musk on themselves; they spray their leftover food also, to keep others from eating it, and always stain themselves when they are caught in a trap." Ross was wonderful in just random reminiscence. I wish I could remember his actual speech. Ross knows a lot about words.

Most of our talk was about the trail and the scarcity of food. I told one of the stories I had heard over on the west shore, concerning the starvation of some Caribou Eskimos there in 1926. A whole family lived in the interior during that very hard winter and could find no caribou. The youngest child died first and was buried. Then the father, then the older son, and then the mother died, and all remained unburied because the survivors were too weak for any tasks. At last the sole survivor of the family, a very young girl, found herself with a knife in

199

her hand, standing above the still warm body of her mother. In her starved state, the girl was apparently more than half-mad. She must have eaten the mother's meat. Then she cut all the meat off all the other unburied corpses, and with renewed strength loaded that food onto the family sled. Living on the meat of her load, she managed somehow to get out toward the Bay and to reach an Eskimo encampment. The load of human flesh on the sled horrified the other natives. They drove her away from their settlement and into the snow again. When she reached another camp, word of her deeds had preceded her. Again she was an outcast. No natives would receive her. She came at last to the Mountie at Chesterfield Inlet with her story. He believed the tale and took pity on her, finding some work that let her live near the post. Mountie Joyce, then on duty at Chesterfield Inlet, later told the whole tale to me.

Ross shook his head, impressed. He admitted that he had heard no east-coast story quite gory enough to match it.

Ross is a strong advocate of light weights on the trail and of food that is easy to prepare. He mixes fish cakes and meat cakes, cooks them, lets them freeze, and simply thaws them out as they are needed. "The worst thing you can take into the North is a frying pan," he insisted. "Everything should be boiled." By drinking the juice, of course, one retains all the nourishment. He was sure that we should have done better to have packed all our food into mealtime small lots and deposited the lots in separate caches all along the way. We could have done this in summer, by means of canoes, and then gone in in winter, comparatively unhindered, in our present way. Doutt and I politely listened. Ross was almost always right, but our two raided food deposits in the interior had not left us open-minded on the subjects of caches.

But why had he wanted us to take Daniel in particular into the interior? That tale he told us almost the last of all. Daniel Petacumeshcum was not a Hudson's Bay

Company hunter. He had lately been cajoled into selling his furs to a local free-trader. It was, of course, to Ross' advantage to have the good Company hunters left behind to attend to their traps. Daniel was competent and able as a guide—on that score we had no kick coming, and we could not quite forget, in fairness, that it was Daniel who finally shot the first seal. Nevertheless, we were not fond of Daniel, and there had been one dangerous moment.

On the night when the first seal meat had been divided, the Indians had ignorantly made a bag out of the skin in which to carry the blubber away. When Doutt saw it, he probably had horrible visions of having the precious skin go to pieces. With eloquent gestures he himself began unloading it, but with an even more eloquent gesture, Daniel grabbed for the axe. The other Indians intervened, but we all had been frightened. (In the Indians' country, Ross interrupted to explain, the hunter himself owns all of his kill—even the skin of it.) It was lucky, indeed, that our George was such a diplomat. Eventually he had been able to work things out our way. Doutt himself had once been admirably tactful, simply by pretending, when things were at an impasse, to be taking the vain Daniel Petacumeshcum's picture!

Ross' best story was of Mary Took-a-Look's lover, a half-breed, part white and part Indian, whom Ross had been very anxious to send inland with us.

"You remember the night that Mary Took-a-Look rushed outdoors, weeping?" Ross asked, and we remembered. "That was the night," said Ross, "when I told her that I intended to fire the half-breed if he ever showed up again at the post!"

The half-breed had a pathetic story. He was strong and adventurous. He spoke three languages—English, the Cree dialect of the east coast and east coast Husky. He was well qualified for the fur business. The Hudson's Bay Company had sent him over to the Belchers for training under Bob's patient hand, but the Belcher Eskimos hated the strange Indian and the half-breed complicated

201

matters by falling in love with Bob's young Eskimo cook. Her name was Mata, and although only a child, she was the reigning queen of the Belchers. She scorned the half-breed, who grew more and more unhappy. He was already lonely on the islands, with no other Indians to visit and the only white man his unbending superior. Among the natives at Moose Factory the talented half-breed had been the most popular bachelor, indeed the "toast of the town." It was all Bob could do to keep him sane until August.

Bob returned the half-breed to the mainland on the August supply boat and Ross put him to work at Great Whale River. There he took the fancy of Ross' cook, the Eskimo Mary Took-a-Look. But the half-breed treated her much as he had been treated by Mata on the Belcher Islands. He seemed to move in a great circle of misery.

He was moody and useless at the post, and Ross, partly in punishment and partly for convenience, ordered him to take the dog sled and one of the geologists and make the long and tiresome trip down to Moose Factory— some 250 miles. The trip down, with a companion, no load and facing homeward, would not give the half-breed such a really bad time of it. The trip back, alone, with a heavy load of provisions was intended for the punishment.

Even before our start inland, the sled had been gone for a month. Day after day Ross looked for the half-breed to come into the post ground, contrite and willing after the bitter weeks alone on the trail. But when he finally came, he was roaring drunk. He had finished the last drop of whisky from the next year's medical supplies, and he hadn't the faintest idea where he had been in the meantime.

Mary Took-a-Look was broken-hearted when Ross fired the half-breed. The Indian had tried to recoup his fortunes by following Doutt and me clear to Richmond Gulf, but beyond the Gulf he hadn't dared to try to find us. The particulars are missing after that. Eventually, no doubt, the half-breed found himself back home at Moose Factory, and came to the end of his strange Ungava interlude.

"I suppose," said Bob lightly, as we discussed my specimens, "it wouldn't hurt me to know a little more about birds. . . ."

EPILOGUE

Appropriately, Twomey ends the Ungava quest back at the Great Whale River post with an exchange of anecdotes and stories, as if to begin immediately to make the experience into a narrative. And, also in keeping with many of the classic models, the returned travellers soon embarked on a new adventure. The party had reached the post on 8 April; on 10 April they left to cross the ice-bridge, arriving on the third day at the Belcher Islands. And, two days after the crossing was completed the ice-bridge cracked and widened at one point, quickly becoming impassable for another year. Twomey and Doutt remained on the Belchers from April until September, gathering scientific data. Bob Cruikshank, the manager of the post at Tukarak, did learn more about the birds, just as he anticipated in the conversation at the end of the Ungava part of the story. Some time later Cruikshank was to appear at the Carnegie Museum in Pittsburgh where he turned over his extensive and painstakingly made catalogue of the autumn bird migration on the Belchers, thus completing the record Dr. Twomey had begun in the spring.

Two brief accounts of the Ungava expedition preceded the publication of *Needle to the North*: J. Kenneth Doutt, "The Expedition to Hudson Bay," *Carnegie Magazine*, XII (January 1939), 227-36 and Arthur C. Twomey, "Ungava Expedition," *The Beaver*, Outfit 270 (June 1939), 44-49. In both the article and the book

Twomey was careful not to trespass on Doutt's work by providing too much information about the seal and its significance. He contented himself with affirming that *kasagea* is not *netchek*, reminding the reader that a full description was not possible in his popular account, but would have to wait until the publication of the scientific paper. The scientific account did appear soon after: see J. Kenneth Doutt, "A Review of the Genus *Phoca*," *Annals of the Carnegie Museum*, XXIX (1942-43), 61-125. There Doutt proclaimed: "This paper announces the discovery of a new race of *Phoca vitulina* from Seal Lake, Ungava." Not concerned solely with the biology of seals, this extensive article includes fourteen plates, several maps, information about the trip, a history of the exploration of the region and various other details which supplement Twomey's book. Doutt, of course, mostly compared the Ungava subspecies of the seal (which he named *Phoca vitulina mellonae* in honour of Mr. and Mrs. William Larimer Mellon who helped finance the expedition) with other groups and races of the genus *Phoca*. Doutt's view was that the subspecies discovered at Seal Lakes had been isolated for at least four thousand years.

A later article questions Doutt's claims about the Ungava seal as a separate subspecies and the length of its isolation: see Arthur W. Mansfield, "Distribution of the Harbour Seal, *Phoca vitulina linnaeus*, in Canadian Arctic Waters," *Journal of Mammalogy*, XLVIII (1967), 249-57. Mansfield presents evidence to show that such characteristics as the angle of the jaw, brought forward by Doutt as a distinctive feature, are not unusual, and can be found in other specimens. Further, Mansfield argues that fresh-water seals are not unique, and that access to Lower Seal Lake might have been gained by a relatively recent migration up the Leaf River from Ungava Bay.

After all, does it matter? Does it matter that *Phoca vitulina mellonae* may not be a subspecifically distinct race? Does it matter that this supposedly land-locked race may not have been isolated in the Seal Lakes of Ungava for thousands of years? Such questions are of course important to biologists, and rightly so. But new discoveries have always had a way of consigning old discoveries to the dustbin of history. For the reader of *Needle to the North* the status of *kasagea*, the mythic seal of the Ungava lakes, is secure: we know that *kasagea* is not *netchek*. And we also know that *kasagea* may be attained only after the most arduous of journeys, taken in midwinter, with the special knowledge of the right assistants and guides, upon completion of a period of patient waiting, and only after coming through the requisite tests and ordeals.

W.C.J.

NOTES

[1]The Temiskaming and Northern Ontario Railway from Cochrane to Moosonee was completed in 1932. The present town of Moosonee had its beginnings in 1903 with the establishment of a trading-post by the Revillon Frères, set up to rival the Hudson's Bay Company post on Moose Factory Island.

[2]The Ontario Northland Transportation Commission's excursion train, the "Polar Bear Express," now travels from Cochrane to Moosonee in less than five hours. The bush from Mile 49.3 to Mile 52 was part of a 30,000-acre area destroyed by a forest fire in June 1976.

[3]A *tupek* is an Eskimo tent. A full description is given on p. 102 below.

[4]Twomey forgivably exaggerates the size of this building, which served for years as store, provision shed and trading-room. Erected in the nineteenth century and still standing in the nineteen-forties, its dimensions, as recorded in a plan of the post drawn in 1895, were 54 by 25 feet (Hudson's Bay Company Archives, Provincial Archives of Manitoba, B372/e/7, Plan GWR Post 1895).

[5]The facts about Harold (whose surname is usually spelled Udgaarden or Udgaarten) vary. Flaherty refers to him as "half-Indian, half-Swede" (*My Eskimo Friends,* p. 13). Whereas Twomey estimated his age as "about 80" in 1938, John J. Honigmann said he was 74 in 1949 (see *Social Networks in Great Whale River*, National Museum of Canada Bulletin No. 178 [Ottawa: Department of Northern Affairs and Natural Resources, 1962], p. 7., note 2). Honigmann states that Harold's father, who "may have come to Canada from Norway," married a woman whose mother was Cree and whose father may have been Métis. A note in *The Beaver* of December 1932 announced that Harold had just retired from the Company after 49 years' service, that he was born at Moose Factory in 1867, that he was of Scandinavian descent and that he went to Great Whale in 1892 and had never been south since (pp. 177-78). Honigmann says that Harold died on 3 April, 1950. His wife, Mary, sister of Husky Bill and Nero Fleming, survived him. Harold was certainly never a Hudson's Bay Company "factor" in the strict sense. While he did fill in as post manager from time to time, most of his employment at the Great Whale River post was as a labourer and interpreter.

[6]Twomey gives Harold's age as "about 80." He was actually in his early seventies at this time, assuming *The Beaver* was correct in placing his birthdate as 1867. For Flaherty's description of Harold's house, see *My Eskimo Friends*, pp. 13-14.

206

[7]In *My Eskimo Friends* it is her husband, Old Harold, who "sat beside her, embarrassed and ill at ease, gazing into space, and silent" (p. 14).

[8]Fort George is the closest settlement down the coast from Great Whale River, and Rupert's House is between Fort George and Moose Factory. Twomey's wording, which has Rupert's House first and then Fort George, has been altered here.

[9]The taste of the meat was a major difference between *kasagea* and *netchek* mentioned by three Inuit men in conversation with me at Great Whale River in February 1982. It was accounted for by the different diet of the fresh-water seal.

[10]This is the third time that Twomey refers to a "Jeff" (see pp. 53-54), which seems to be an affectionate nickname for Roy Jeffries.

[11]This statement is probably a good deal too sweeping, and at other places in the narrative Twomey recognizes that scarcity of game as well as shortage of ammunition can cause hardship. Lewis G. Maver, an earlier post manager at Great Whale River, described how his party came close to starvation on a trip from Fort George to Great Whale—in fact, three men died after reaching their destination from the effects of the ordeal. They had lots of ammunition and expert native hunters along, but the fact that there was little game to be had, not even birds, coupled with adverse weather, led to great difficulties. At camp after camp along the way the story was the same. Maver concludes: "Take a rifle? Yes, by all means; but also a good supply of food when travelling along the coast of Hudson Bay" ("Near Starvation on Hudson Bay," *The Beaver*, July 1923, pp. 367-72).

[12]According to a sketch-map made by Daniel Petacumeshcum (presumably with dates added by J.K. Doutt) the party was camped at the western end of Clearwater Lake on 7 March, across the bay on the other side of the outlet for the Clearwater River on 8 March, and at the eastern end of the lake on 9 March (see J. Kenneth Doutt, "A Review of the Genus *Phoca*," *Annals of the Carnegie Museum*, XXIX [1942-43], 78). This discrepancy in dates and locations is probably due to the difficulties of keeping track of dates in the midst of terrain that looked the same day after day, as well as problems encountered in reconstructing camp notes later.

[13]The Anglican Church has been present on the Ungava coast for well over a century and from the earliest days has trained native catechists (as Ekumiak and Daniel seem to have been). As Honigmann noted from his observations at Great Whale River in 1949: "Sunday is marked by the firm avoidance of several activities: work (including hunting), playing ball and other games (no harm if children play, but adults should refrain), buying and selling, and travelling. It is permitted to fetch water on the holy day, and should

food in camp be lacking, there is no harm in hunting on Sunday. In fact, a Sunday hunt undertaken out of need is likely to be especially successful" (*Social Networks in Great Whale River*, p. 68). It is doubtful that the Indians would have travelled on Sunday even if Daniel had not been present.

[14]Twomey has "due east" here. As Doutt's "Reconnaissance Survey" map (included as Plate XIV with his article) shows, the direction taken was due west from the east shore of Clearwater Lake to the large island (Gumpsch-gu-dan-a-gow Island).

[15]On another occasion "the old chief" is referred to as "Rupert's father." According to John Kawapit (in conversation with Mrs. Andrew Wetmore at Great Whale River, March 1982), Jacob Rupert's father had no given name; he was simply "Rupert." And Jacob had a brother, significantly older than him, whose name was John. Mr. Kawapit could not recall anyone by the name of George Rupert.

John Kawapit, one of the elders in the Cree community regarded highly for his wisdom, has a personal connection with Jacob Rupert. His daughter married Jacob's son; and, as Honigmann reports, in 1949 the families of Jacob Rupert and John Kawapit shared the same household, living in two adjoining tents (*Social Networks in Great Whale River,* pp. 53-54).

[16]There are difficulties here, both in the original text and in Ross' meaning. First, Norman Ross seems to have been stationed at the *HBC* post at Neoskweskau (which Twomey spells "Neaquesa"), located in the general area referred to ("300 miles up the Rupert River"). Characteristically, Twomey has "Swampy Crees" here, which has been emended, as elsewhere, to "Eastern Crees." Then, in the following sentence, Twomey has: "Ross told tales of death at Neapasha." "Neapasha," which cannot otherwise be located, has been taken as another reference to "Neaquesa" and emended to "Neoskweskau" once again.

The issue under discussion, apparently, is how to place the Richmond Gulf Indians in relation to other groups of Indians in the Quebec-Labrador peninsula. Ross' opinion seems to be that the Indians of the Richmond Gulf were not the Naskapi of the north ("Ungava tribe Indians"), but that they should be considered as belonging to the Eastern Cree. His view is based on the similarity of their songs and chants, as well as of their death practices, with those of the Indians he knew at Neoskweskau.